There is Nothing New Under the Sun

There is Nothing New Under the Sun

Robert E. Leverenz

RESOURCE *Publications* • Eugene, Oregon

THERE IS NOTHING NEW UNDER THE SUN

Copyright © 2015 Robert E. Leverenz. All rights reserved. Except for brief quotations in critical publications or reviews, no part of this book may be reproduced in any manner without prior written permission from the publisher. Write: Permissions. Wipf and Stock Publishers, 199 W. 8th Ave., Suite 3, Eugene, OR 97401.

Resource Publications
An Imprint of Wipf and Stock Publishers
199 W. 8th Ave., Suite 3
Eugene, OR 97401

www.wipfandstock.com

ISBN 13: 978-1-4982-2430-7

Manufactured in the U.S.A.   11/09/2015

Contents

Introduction | vii

Historical Note | 1
The Meeting of the Past and Present | 1
The Pride of Power | 3
The Vietnam War | 5
Suicide | 7
The Death Penalty | 10
The Peace Movement | 13
"Make My Day" | 15
Homosexuality | 18
Dress to Kill | 21
The Statue of Liberty | 23
Violence/The Survival Game | 26
America—A Very Religious Nation | 29
Geraldine Ferraro | 31
Another First/Not the Last | 31
The Recovery of Imagination | 33
Can the Children of Isaac and Ishmael live in peace? | 35
Cynicism | 38
Auschwitz: The Holocaust and Remembering | 40
Martin Niemoeller | 43
Intolerance | 46
Violence and Guns | 49
Smile and Say Cheese* | 53
Patriotism* | 55
Fear* | 57
The Rise and Fall of the Religious Right | 59
Disinformation* | 62
Bumper Stickers & Prejudice* | 64

Contents

Baseball Revisited* | 66
Can the Traditional Family be Saved? | 68
"To Burn or Not to Burn"* | 72
A State of Minds* | 73
Conclusion | 75

* "Stand Alone" commentaries from the 80's.

Introduction
There is nothing new under the sun!

Truer words have never been spoken!! In the event anyone reading this is not familiar with the title, it is from the Hebrew Scripture and it has endured millennium.

> "What has been is what will be and what has been done is what will be done. There is nothing new under the sun."
> Ecclesiastes 1:9

In addition to Ecclesiastes we can add the familiar words of George Santayana to set the stage. "Those who cannot remember the past are condemned to repeat it." The wisdom of George Santayana is validated by the movements of history as well as that of the Preacher of Ecclesiastes.

George Santayana was born 16 December 1863 in Madrid, Spain. He died 26 September 1952 in Rome Italy. A Spanish born American author Santayana became a philosopher, essayist, poet and novelist.

As I read and juxtaposed some of the major issues of the 1980's and the fact they are still with us 30 years later I began to wonder if we can or if we have learned from the past. George Santayana's insight provides a response to my wondering. We have not learned from the past in most instances. This will become clear as the review of the issues examined will prove.

Historical Note

During my tenure at St. Timothy United Methodist Church, Cedar Falls, Iowa, between the years 1982 and 1987 I had the privilege of providing commentaries for public radio operating out of the University of Northern Iowa.

I revisited those commentaries recently in preparation for my book, "That is What They Are in For". Recording those over KUNI was one of the many privileges which came to this pastor.

Looking more closely at those commentaries I realized that many of the issues read as though they appeared in today's New York Times: suicide, gun violence, women's rights and homosexuality. Also spanning the decades are dynamics of human relationships such as intolerance, abuse of power, arrogance, fear and cynicism.

No doubt the relationship between the 80's and the second decade of the 21st century has been addressed at great length by historians and most certainly by journalists. That notwithstanding it is my intention to look at these cultural expressions found in the decades of the 80's and the second decade of the 21st century to test the accuracy of "The Preacher" in Ecclesiastes to see if the drama surrounding these issues is still being played out in the public arena and if there is indeed "nothing new under the sun". Have we learned from the past?

In the recording of these commentaries I have discovered some are simply "stand alone" commentaries. No 21st century parallels come readily to mind. Some are included because they contain an autobiographical note. An example of that would be my discovering baseball once again. Hopefully all will prove interesting to the reader.

The Meeting of the Past and Present
The process informing these commentaries

That brings us to the moment (2014–2015) which I have identified as an age of polarities. This is obvious to all who take time to view

There is Nothing New Under the Sun

the politics of the times, particularly since the historic election of President Barack Obama in 2008. At its best, the political process should result in a synthesis bringing together opposing views, or a compromise between divergent views. Unfortunately a synthesis is rarely reached on significant issues of the day such as the role of the gun in our lives, the death penalty, excellence in education, immigration, war and peace, suicide, violence, and the "abuse of power".

Should my literary effort require such I'm identifying the polarized groups as progressives and reactionaries or one can say liberals and conservatives. Nationally these groups are typically, the Democrats and Republicans respectively. Those are categories to which we can attach some cursory understanding. However, as a theologian I must remember the counsel of the monastic Thomas Merton, theologian and biblical scholar who reminds us that we are made in the image of God. He calls upon Christ followers to see beyond the categories of the market place and view all as human being possessing within the divine.

As these issues and concepts of the 80's are played out in the second decade of the 21st century the players may have changed but the similarity of positions stand in stark relief.

Since these issues span the decades there seems to be some dynamics embedded in human DNA. These dynamics appear to be almost archetypal: fear, arrogance of power, deceit, cynicism, patriotism, totalitarianism, xenophobia, need for a scapegoat, outrage and imagination to name a few. They make it possible for the Preacher to proclaim with accuracy: "There is nothing new under the sun," and for the statement of George Santayana centuries later to confirm the Preacher's insight.

Beside the common ground between the 80's and 2014, a new awareness, a new reality has become apparent: globalization. This reality finds expression in the areas of communication, commerce, education, hunger, diseases, cultural expressions such as movies, and finally with the globalization of terror and grief.

The internet brings to our attention the struggles in the global community: Burma, Israel and Palestine, the horrors in Nigeria, Somalia, Sudan, South Sudan, Kenya, Ukraine, the Middle

The Pride of Power

East, Egypt, and Syria to name a few. We observe the independent movements in Scotland resulting in the Scots choosing to remain in the U.K. with a vote September 18, 2014, and Catalonia where a recent vote to "break away" from Spain was postponed. In the past we have read of the rumblings in the province of Quebec as some advocate the establishment of a separate country. Globalization has brought us great advances in the field of medicine and a variety of health issues.

That being said is it possible for us to learn from the past? Has our global awareness shown that we have learned from the past? I have serious doubts but I can hope because we have become "one neighborhood" in which much has become global in its impact. Perhaps progress can be made in minimizing the impact and the frequency with which the inflicting of cruelty on one another takes place. Let us begin to explore the "then" and in many cases the "now".

It is helpful to remember the administration referred to in many of these commentaries covers the presidency of Ronald Reagan.

THEN
The Pride of Power
November 26, 1986

From the Greek tragedians and theologians of today such as Reinhold Niebuhr comes sound advice for the members of the National Security team; the President and members of his administration.

The Heroes of Greek tragedy were always counselled to remember their mortality and to escape retribution by observing power restraints. The issue before the heroes of Greek tragedy and theologians is that of Pride which St. Augustine defined as "undue exaltation."

Niebuhr tells us about the pride of power. He writes:

> "There is a pride of power in which the human ego assumes its self-sufficiency and self-mastery. It imagines itself secure against all difficulties. . . .It believes itself to

There is Nothing New Under the Sun

be the author of its own existence, the judge of its own values, and the master of its own destiny."

It appears that this administration has never learned or it has forgotten the counsel of the Greeks and theologians. But in the light of day this basic lesson concerning the use of power is being learned.

If there is one word that has characterized this administration, it has been the word arrogance. That word is appropriate in identifying the posture the prideful ones have towards the world.

It is essential the investigations continue and the truth be made known, but an appreciation of the human condition might be useful for the critics of this administration as well for another dimension of this is the pride of virtue. It is not difficult for the pride of virtue to become the pride of self-righteousness.

Niebuhr speaks to the situation once again:

> "Moral pride is the pretension of finite man that his highly conditioned virtue is the final righteousness and that his very relative moral standards are absolute."

If possible, the moral and the good have to be seen in some objective light by some objective standards which bring judgment upon all pronouncements and actions by all political parties. The critics as well as the perpetrators of illegal or immoral acts possess the pride of power and the pride of virtue.

What everyone in position of authority needs is to have inscribed on his or her desk is this statement by Bertrand Russell.

> "Every man would like to be God if it were possible. Some few find it difficult to admit the impossibility."
> (Nature and Destiny of Many, page 189)

Poindexter, North, Reagan, Bush; perhaps you and I to name a few, might heed the warning given to the heroes of Greek tragedy and the directives of theologians and philosophers, as well as the popular belief: "Pride goes before a fall."

Vietnam War Memorial

NOW

President Obama in Brussels, Belgium
March 29, 2014

President Obama spoke to NATO allies about the inappropriate attempt on the part of the President of Russia, Vladimir Putin to annex territory in Crimea and the Ukraine. Boundaries cannot be redrawn. Nor can we exercise our military muscle in that region as once thought. Alas, there are those in positions of power in this country as well as abroad who have not accepted that reality. The self-serving myth of "American Exceptionalism" feeds our national hubris. From Vietnam to Iraq and Afghanistan the pride of power has found expression. In recent speeches in New Hampshire Republican candidates for the 2016 presidential election played the theme song of "American Exceptionalism". This was noted in the New York Times of April 23rd.

THEN

Vietnam War Memorial
Paramount Park, Waterloo, Iowa
September 26, 1986

On Saturday, September 20th, a Vietnam War Memorial was dedicated at Paramount Park, Waterloo. Inscribed on its granite surface are the names of 45 young men from Black Hawk County who died in that war.

As I thought about that memorial and the war, I found myself sharing some of the reflections expressed by the people at that dedication: anger, concern that we might forget that war, that the men and women who participated in that war were not fully appreciated by the citizenry, particularly by the critics of that tragedy.

As I remembered a young friend of mine who died there, my anger and concern focused on the deceit practiced by our government in the executing of that war from its beginning to its conclusion. Particularly appalling to me was the political expediency

There is Nothing New Under the Sun

which dictated the actions of the Senate leadership in 1964 when they passed the Gulf of Tonkin Resolution.

This political expediency was confessed by J. W. Fulbright, the Chairman of the Senate Foreign Relations Committee. This confession appears in his book, "The Arrogance of Power". It is worth repeating.

As Chairman of the Foreign Relations Committee, I served as floor manager of the Southeast Asia resolution and did all I could to bring about its prompt and overwhelming adoption. I did so because I was confident President Johnson would use our endorsement with wisdom and restraint. I was also influenced by partisanship: and election campaign was in progress and I had no wish to make any difficulties for the President in his race against a Republican candidate whose election I thought would be a disaster for the country. My role in the adoption of the resolution of August 7, 1964, is a source of neither pleasure nor pride for me today." (Page 52)

Congress shares the blame for that tragic act of political expediency and partisanship by J. W. Fulbright.

In an interview with a writer of the Waterloo Courier, Mr. Carl Rogers, whose son Craig was killed in Vietnam is quoted as saying: "I think there's an attempt to forget about the whole thing", to forget about the war.

If there is one thing we must do it is to remember not only the tragic consequences of an ill-conceived policy, but the political component in the passage of The Gulf of Tonkin Resolution of August 7, 1964.

As we think of the policies of this administration towards the people of Nicaragua, it would be helpful for the people of this nation to note carefully the PARTISAN nature of the votes supporting our funding of the Contras and the inflicting of pain on the people of Nicaragua. When the votes are as partisan as they have been, the distinct impression is given that political expediency is the prevailing motive for such votes and not whether the cause is just or meritorious.

Suicide

With respect, we remember those who served and died in the Vietnam War. We do honor to their memory by challenging the administration and its supporters whose policy is initiated and supported by political expediency and PARTISAN POLITICS.

NOW
Five years of war
Iraq and Afghanistan

"When will they ever learn..." so goes the refrain of the ballad by Pete Seeger, "Where Have All the Flowers Gone". The dictum by George Santayana looms large on the pages of today's "history in the making. We have not learned the stories of history. Nor has our government taken care of our veterans. Protests are minimal in part because Americans are not feeling the pain acutely. The draft is not in place thus muting protest. The impact of these wars appears to be minimal. Add to this the limited number of troops involved in our current "drone warfare" the lessons of the past recede into the historical landscape. There is something immoral about "drone warfare", death raining down on people in the hills directed by a technician thousands of miles away free from any risk.

THEN
Suicide
September 1986

The issue of suicide, specifically teenage suicide has been making the news again, appropriately so. This issue has been brought to our attention by two recently released studies dealing with the connection between television, news program or features dealing with suicide and teenage suicide.

These studies conclude that there is a noticeable increase in teenage suicide following the airing of television, movies, features or news reports about suicide. It seems that teenagers practice what is called "imitative behavior." Offsetting this conclusion is

There is Nothing New Under the Sun

the premise: no one knows how many teen age suicides have been deterred by these same movies, features and news reports.

As we think about these studies and about the issue of suicide in the adult population as well, it might be helpful to direct our thoughts to the survivors of this tragedy. Although this reality might be better served in conversation and dialogue a commentary on this might be helpful if for no other reason than that it might promote conversation.

The survivors of suicides are overwhelmed with guilt and anger. They question their personal role in the death of this loved one or friend. They create what Fr. Pangrazzi calls "rescue fantasies." "If only…if only…" They experience anger, feel cheated or rejected by their loved ones. Some survivors express this as follows:

"Didn't we mean anything to him?" or "She probably didn't love me because she didn't think I was worth living for." And again, "I never felt so close to my brother and then he pulls this on me."

In addition to this, they experience a perceived "social stigma." Neighbors stay away for fear of saying the wrong thing.

In response to these feelings of guilt and anger and being stigmatized, the survivors need to be surrounded by compassion and understanding. They need permission to talk about their feelings. They might be led to understand that the reality of suicide can happen to anyone… anyone.

We have to accept our limitations in these circumstances. As we think of the "rescue fantasies", survivors have to be helped to see that in the last analysis we cannot choose for another, even though we might be able to influence another to a degree. But ultimately the choice is theirs.

Not even love is enough sometimes to save another's life.

Survivors have to be helped to begin to take care of themselves, to reaffirm their own goodness and be led back to hope. The best thing we can do is to try to help prevent suicide by listening, taking people seriously when they speak of it and seek help. But when a suicide occurs, teenage or adult, what is required of us is to surround the survivor with understanding, compassion and a caring presence.

Suicide

NOW
March 2014/2015

On the Washington Mall 223 America flags stand as a testimony to the number of service personnel who have committed suicide as the legacy of our current wars in Iraq and Afghanistan. The high rate of suicide among service personnel is linked to what is called PTSD—Post Traumatic Stress Disorder attributed to the horrors of war. The observations in 1986 seem to be relevant today as well.

Another dimension of suicide has surfaced in recent years although the reality of such has been present far longer. That reality is a new expression of teenage suicide focusing on the young person's sexual orientation. Studies have shown us that teenage suicide is the leading age group in the social milieu and gay teen age suicide is most prominent in that group. Bullying of gay young people has been in the headlines the last few years. Not long ago in eastern Oregon a young teen took his own life. From that tragedy his father sought to walk across the United States speaking about the subject. Tragically, he was hit by a truck in Colorado and subsequently died.

The manner in which we face the reality can be informed by our understanding in 1986. For teens and service people, the turbulent times in which we live continues to make this personal tragedy a very present reality. In recent days we have become aware of the number of suicides of transgender young people. Perhaps awareness can be met with understanding, compassion and acceptance and our transgender friends will not be driven to despair and suicide. Also in the July 27, 2015 issue of the New York Times an article focused on the reality of suicides at the undergraduate level at our universities. It dealt at length with the pressurized milieu under which high performing students live. In the last 13 months there were six suicides at the University of Pennsylvania, Tulane registered 4, Appalachian State at least three—Cornell faced six suicides in the 2009-10 academic year. In 2003-4, five New York University students leapt to their deaths.

There is Nothing New Under the Sun

THEN
The Death Penalty
December 24, 1982

Greetings ladies and gentlemen! I'm pleased you could be here to witness an event you will never forget. Follow me into this room. As you can see this is an observation room with a one way viewing window. We are about to be spectators at an execution, an event expressing the supreme power of the state to take life. They are conversing. He and the jailer are conversing.

"Mr. Brooks, do you have any last words?"

"Yes, I do. There is no God but Allah. Verily to him we belong and verily unto him do we return."

As you look at Mr. Brooks, note his clothing. He is wearing gold pants, a brown shirt open down the front and black cloth shoes. He has an intravenous needle in his right arm. That tube snakes around behind the curtain where a prison employee is ready to start the flow of a lethal drug. At this moment the employee is injecting the drug into the tube. Mr. Brooks is quite still, his eyes closed, as though he is sleeping. He is beginning to move. He is gasping and wheezing for breath. Gasping and wheezing. . . . Now he is still.

That man bending over him is Dr. Gray, the prison doctor. He is about to speak. "I pronounce this man dead."

For the sixth time since 1976, the state, the government has validated the idea of revenge. Capital punishment has been applied once more. Civilization is dehumanized once again. My friends, if you want the opportunity to be the recipient of the death penalty as it is applied so unfairly in this country your chances are much greater if you are poor, if you are a member of the minority groups in this country and if you have no influence in the community. How do I know? Let me tell you!

Remember two names: John Spenkelink and Dan White.

In 1972 John Spenkelink was electrocuted in Starke, Florida for killing a drifter. A few months later Dan White was given a

The Death Penalty

seven years sentence for killing Mayor Moscone of San Francisco and councilman Harvey Milk; a double homicide by a supervisor.

Dan White was an all American male capable of hiring counsel received seven years. But the poor man with little education and no influence was put to death.

Currently (1982) there are 1056 people on death row across the nation. 45% of these are black. 80% of the death row population is in the South. Florida alone has 150 people on death row. The South has gained an unenviable label: "The Death Belt."

Even the most hard core advocates of capital punishment can see the disparities in the application of the death penalty. And yet, we persist in enacting laws to reinstate it. At this reading currently 38 states have such laws on the books. Iowa does not. Iowa is still an island of civility and decency on this issue. It has been so since 1965 when the death penalty was repealed when Harold Hughes was governor. As long as Robert Ray was in the governor's chair, the death penalty had little chance of being restored. But now...?

NOW
April 5, 2014

Missouri and Oklahoma are currently in difficulty with obtaining the drug necessary to carry out executions by lethal injection. Oregon, under the leadership of Governor Kitzhaber (an emergency room physician), will not be carrying out executions. He categorically stated none will be carried out under his watch. As of March 2015 his successor Governor Kate Brown has continued his policy. Currently 32 states and the federal government permit capital punishment. The innocent project has exonerated 173 death row inmates. Their innocence has been proven. I would like to believe the death penalty will be banned totally in the United States. The European Union has banned it from its member nations.

The Pew Research Center and Death Penalty Information Center reports the fact that death penalty support has declined since it was reinstated in 1976. It peaked in 1999 at 98 executions.

There is Nothing New Under the Sun

In 2013 there were 39. In 2014 as of April 30th there were 20 executions with another 14 scheduled. Thirty two states no longer have capital punishment. Perhaps the remaining 18 states will follow the trend and eliminate the death penalty altogether. On May 27, 2015, Nebraska abolished the death penalty. Now there are 19 states which have abolished the death penalty.

The New York Times last week reported on the death penalty's enforcement in Texas. The headline screamed at the reader proclaiming "Texas prides itself on executing the death penalty efficiently". In recent days in Arizona it took 2 hours for a man to die of lethal injection. One wonders about the "...cruel and unusual punishment" clause in the U. S. Constitution.

As a student of theology I hold the position that the sanctity of human life is diminished by executing an individual. The theological position I claim is called

"Incarnational theology." This affirms the indwelling of Christ in everyone and challenges the idea that we have the right to take the life of another, individually or by the state representing society at large.

The poet John Donne addresses the diminishment of all by one person's death.

No Man is an Island

No man is an island
Entire to itself.
Every man is a part of the continent
A part of the main.

If a clod be washed away by the sea
Europe is the less,
As well as if a promontory were
As well as if a manor of thy friends'
Or of thine own were.
Any man's death diminishes me,
Because I am involved in mankind,
And therefore never send to know

The Peace Movement

For whom the bell tolls,
It tolls for thee.

John Donne, Poet, Priest, Lawyer
b. 22 January 1572
d. 31 March 1631

THEN
The Peace Movement
Nuclear Weapons

"May I infect you with a disease?" This message was sent to the English in the late 1960's by their Dutch neighbors across the channel. It was an invitation to join them in raising their voices against the nuclear arms race.

With that invitation we saw the spread of a malady of conscience. That contagion has spread from London through the capitals of Europe: Amsterdam, Bonn, Stockholm, Oslo, Copenhagen, Paris, Brussels, Rome, Madrid, and others.

It proved infectious to Eastern Europe as well finding expression in Romania, Hungary, and East Germany. It surfaced in Japan and the United States. What began inauspiciously with an invitation from the Dutch Interchurch Peace Council (IKV) has sent ripples across the globe culminating in a tidal wave of concern washing against the buildings of the United Nations. Perhaps this tidal wave of concern will bring to reality the dream engraved on the walls of the United Nations building; the dream of a day when people will "beat their swords into plowshares, and their spears into pruning hooks; a day when nation shall not lift of sword against nation and neither shall they learn war anymore..." (Isaiah 2:4)

Presidential Directive of 1980, #59 proclaimed that the U. S. targeting policy would also include Soviet and East European military sites in the possibility of a "limited nuclear war."

President Reagan's careless remarks about a nuclear exchange in Europe without such a conflict escalating to the superpower level, was profoundly disturbing to Europeans. It added impetus to the peace movement. People became terrified of the idea of being the battleground between east and west.

What is the impact of this infectious disease called "Hollanditis?" Will it be short lived? Is this "Hollanditis" a plague destined to take on epidemic proportions?

How do we diagnose this? At this reading, three voices of world powers have registered responses to the demonstration at the U. N. Our Secretary of Defense has stated that this large turnout was unlikely to have any direct impact on administrative policy. On the other hand, Chancellor Helmut Schmidt in his speech of June 14th said the peace movement brings to the disarmament conference a moral force.

The USSR has said it would not be the first to launch a nuclear attack. This statement is viewed with skepticism by the U. S. Our government says if we promised the same, the "nuclear umbrella", as it is called, would be removed from Europe making it vulnerable to Soviet conventional attack. Apparently, the Reagan administration has not heard the voice of the people in Europe questioning that specious reasoning. There is no security in a policy which frightens the citizens it is supposed to protect.

The peace movement has broken the paralyzing feeling of helplessness. If "Hollanditis" can be seen as a malady of the conscience, helplessness can be a malady of the human spirit. When human beings believe themselves to be helpless, helpless they become.

The peace movement has broken the "hex" of the bomb. There is cause for hope.

There is a sense of moral outrage in the land which will continue to spread.

"May I infect you with a disease?" was the greeting from the Dutch. It could be cause for celebration if this "disease" of the conscience will infect the leadership of nations and challenge the "last epidemic" which would come with a nuclear holocaust.

"Make My Day"

NOW

The Peace Movement

The Peace Movement seems to be lying dormant at this writing. With the absence of a draft and thusly mandatory military service, the onus surrounding participating in the military and thus war has been diminished. Aspects of military life have been making the headlines relative to the services of the Veterans Administration for veterans experiencing PTSD. A major issue in the current debate is the ineffective delivery of services to Vets.

Also at this writing President Obama is speaking of creating a new generation of nuclear weapons.

A new dimension has been added to the dimension of warfare: cyber warfare. Alas, we can only wonder if we "have learned anything from history". Cyber warfare does not produce "body bags" at this time, but if enough fear is generated by cyber warfare a "killing field" could be created.

THEN

"Make My Day"
March 27, 1985

I had a dream the other night. It began with this line: "Go ahead, make my day!"

I heard President Reagan say it. He was inviting Congress to pass legislation which would raise billions in tax revenue. As my dream developed Congress did pass a tax increase, some $50 billion would be added to the treasury in the next two years.

The President was elated. Congress did indeed "make his day."

He could now go before the American people, all the American people and tell them immediate efforts were being made to restore much needed domestic programs.

Nutrition programs for pregnant women and the children would receive funds. This could reverse the trend begun in 1980

There is Nothing New Under the Sun

which saw an increase in infant mortality due in large part to cutbacks in federally funded programs.

The President would now be able to tell the people: immunization programs for children would be strengthened. A nationwide system of day care centers would be established to assist the hard pressed employed mothers, particularly single, poor mothers.

The cities would receive revenue sharing funds to breathe new life into their ghettos of death much like the biblical story of the Valley of Dry Bones receiving new life and breath. The environment would be granted a reprieve as money and regulations would put an end to the reign of polluters.

In my dreams billions were given to the Department of Education. They were instructed to strengthen curricula, help pay teacher's' salaries, provide special services to children with special needs.

The Legal Services Corporation received revenue to provide legal assistance to the poor. Equality before the bar of justice became a reality.

Farmers received loans on their spring planting which enabled them to survive.

Money allocated for 42 MX missiles was channeled from those weapons of death to programs of life. A job corps was started to create jobs for the unemployed, particularly for blacks, this group which experiences in some areas 50% unemployment.

The President held a nationally televised news conference to tell the American People, all the people, that Congress had indeed "made his day!" He wanted to thank them.

———

In the midst of the celebration I woke up. I returned to the nightmare of reality.

Farmers were going out of business. Banks were closing. The poor were still being deprived of legal services. Children were still going hungry in this country. Infant mortality rate was on the increase. Schools were being placed in a bind because of a lack of funds. Special services were being cut. Millions of people were

"Make My Day"

coming to the conclusion they were expendable, unneeded, unnecessary and in the way.

As the military consumed our wealth, insecurity became more intense. In the nightmare of reality the environment continued to die. One segment of the country was being pitted against another. Suspicion, fear and hopelessness filled many homes.

In the nightmare of real life, Mr. Reagan continues to be "the little brother of the rich and their political agent" in the words of William Shannon.

Would that Congress had the political will to pick up the challenge thrown down by the President. Would that they would pass legislation to increase taxes and "make the day" for millions of poor people among us: students, farmers, urban dwellers, and most of all the children.

NOW
Budget
April 19, 2014

The statement introducing the commentary of March 27, 1985, "Make My Day" came from the lips of Clint Eastwood as he aimed his 357 Magnum at a criminal, daring him to make a move. The "make my day" scenario addressing the "Dream Budget" found an echoing response in the "standoff" by two prominent individuals. One is Representative Paul Ryan focusing on the Republican federal budget of 2014 which cuts deeply into the safety net of government programs. The challenging voice comes from Pope Francis.

Paul Ryan vs. Pope Francis. The proposed budget by Paul Ryan seeks to cut back billions in food assistance to low income people, cut back in education funds and, support for the states. There is resistance to additional funds to bail out industries, resistance to environmental protection and the providing of funds to support clamping down on industries that pollute like the recent leak in the Charleston River flowing through the capital as well as the rural areas. Who can ignore the melting glaciers, legal aid, refusing to tax the 1% which controls 90% of the wealth, day care centers, and equity in pay for women and men, scholarships to help young people, jobs program for blacks and others…? A year later, March 21, 2015, the budget proposed on this day created by the House of Representatives seeks to cut the same programs as those in 2014. Indeed, "there is nothing new under the sun."

THEN

Homosexuality
1986

Is the homosexual my neighbor? This is more than the title of a book, which it is. It is acknowledgment of a reality. It is a reality which causes fear in the hearts of heterosexuals who do not seek to understand, an intense discomfort for homosexuals who have felt the sting of persecution.

It is estimated that between 5% and 10% of the population is homosexual. When you add to that number their families and friends, there is not a life untouched by the reality of homosexuality. The issue has "come out of the closet", however cautiously and needs to be discussed for the well-being of all.

Although the climate of society has changed somewhat for the better on this issue, we still have a long way to go before the homosexuals among us can be free from fear of persecution, from discrimination in employment, mistreatment at the hands of physicians, deprivation of civil rights, harassment at the hands of certain religious groups, or more painfully, "self-oppression".

The destructive self-oppression by homosexuals was noted in a recent article in "The Des Moines Register." Minnesota District Judge Crane Winton, charged with sexual misconduct spoke of the pain, the loneliness and suppression of the desire to enter into a significant love relationship. Judge Winton said he had resolved to keep his homosexuality a secret to avoid acting upon it and to lead as constructive a life as he could.

Homosexuality

". . . My resolution precluded an open and honest relationship with another man. So it was that when the sense of loneliness became more than I could bear, I sought a form of companionship that I otherwise would not seek." (7/5/82)

In most communities, with few exceptions primarily in larger cities, homosexuals would be harassed and humiliated if their sexual orientation became known. The "Register" article estimated that some 20 million Americans can lose their jobs, lose custody of their children, be discharged from the military or be fined or imprisoned in 26 states because of their sexual orientation. Because of this many wear defensive masks and compromise their integrity in order to survive. Others marry to "look respectable". Marriage becomes a façade behind which one can hide and survive. Who can blame them!!? If I were gay, I too, might want to hide from people who made the following observations.

During the 1977 campaign to abolish the civil rights of homosexuals in Dade County, Florida, a Baptist minister stated that "we are facing the Devil himself in these homosexuals." In the June 6, 1977 issue of "Newsweek", page 22 we find this statement by Jerry Falwell:

". . . so called gay folks (would) just as soon kill you as look at you."

Cars in the area were sporting bumper stickers with motto: "Kill a queer for Christ." (Sunday Register, July 4, 1982)

Perhaps someday we will come to the point where we can be different without having to be considered "bad" or "good". We may discover we do not have to put a value judgment on another, where homosexuality would be considered a variant in human relations and not a sickness or a sin.

But alas, in the midst of our own insecurities, in troubled times, somebody needs to be put down. There will be a need of a scapegoat for society's ills. Someone must be blamed. There is hardly a target better suited for putting down than homosexuals.

Incidentally, to be a homosexual is to be in some pretty important company: Tchaikovsky, Leonard de Vinci, and Michelangelo, Christopher Marlowe, Thomas Gray, King James I (of KJV

There is Nothing New Under the Sun

fame), A. E. Housman, T. E. Lawrence, Walt Whitman, Henry James, Willa Cather and others.

The causes of the fear and hatred surrounding this issue could well be within us and our own uncertainty concerning our sexuality.

Is the Homosexual My Neighbor? Yes he is. Yes she is. Why not get acquainted? This might enable them to be free from one more fear. Perhaps this form of bigotry will become even less "respectable" than it is.

NOW
May 2, 2015

Now marriage opportunities for same sex relationships legal in 19 states and the District of Columbia. Same sex marriage is legal in 20 countries including Spain, France, and now Ireland. Ireland's decision resulted from a public referendum. The Supreme Court of the United States endorsed same sex marriage on June 20, 2015. The policy held by the military towards homosexuals was called "Don't ask, Don't tell." That has been struck down by the Supreme Court. Serving in the military is now acceptable. Some churches and some denominations still lag behind society's granting of full privileges to homosexuals including the United Methodist Church. Most recently, however, The Presbyterian Church USA has extended their definition of marriage to include same-sex couples. Lawsuits have provided protection for gays and lesbians in employment and as the recipients of services in the public arena. However, several states have passed "freedom of religion" laws giving businesses the right to refuse services to individuals on religious grounds. Arkansas and Indiana passed such laws clearly aimed at giving people to discriminate against sexual minorities. The uproar from the business community (Walmart in Arkansas) and the sports community in Indiana (on the eve of the final four in collegiate sports being played in Indianapolis) compelled them to withdraw those laws. Sports figures have "come out" with minimum difficulties. As one processes these changes it would be helpful to read the March 10, 2015 issue of America magazine: "See the Person".

THEN

Dress to Kill
November 9, 1984

Are we dressing our kids to kill?

On Halloween we were visited by children wearing a variety of costumes. One of those visitors caused me to raise the question: "Are we dressing our kids to kill?"

He was fully dressed in jungle fatigues carrying a toy submachine gun. He aimed that gun at me, dressed in a non-scary rabbit costume. I gently pushed the gun aside. He tucked it behind his back. Being a non-speaking rabbit, I gave him the peace sign. He smiled.

The question remains: "Are we dressing our kids to kill?"

A few days later I was reading about James Oliver Huberty. Remember him? He was the man who walked into a McDonald's restaurant in San Ysidro, California carrying three guns, two of them automatic types. He wound up killing 21 people. The newspaper called our attention to the fact that he was wearing jungle camouflage trousers. In addition to that the swat team which finally killed him was wearing jungle camouflage clothing.

As the story of Huberty's life unfolded his neighbors were reported to have said he was "a gun nut who kept mean dogs." One writer, Robert E. Burns in U. S. Catholic raises interesting questions concerning Huberty's clothing.

"I wonder how many of those who did not know Huberty would have thought twice about his wearing camouflage fatigues on an urban street. . . . Huberty's distraught and beleaguered wife had heard him say, "I'm going hunting—hunting for humans." But I doubt that when she took his clothes to the Laundromat she thought it strange that he liked to wear jungle fatigues.

There is Nothing New Under the Sun

With Burns I began to wonder about the necessity of people wearing jungle fatigues in our urban centers, and whether or not these clothes contribute one more ingredient to the climate of violence. What is going on when the general population and not just the Huberty wear jungle fatigues? What is happening when law enforcement officers wear jungle camouflage outfits on urban sidewalks?

I conducted an informal survey in 5 major department stores in the area about jungle fatigues. All five stores say they are popular. Three stores still carry them and plan to continue doing so. No customer or clerk questioned whether jungle fatigues contribute to the climate of violence. All the clerks accept the idea that the kind of clothing one wears does influence the feelings we have about ourselves. But the degree of influence is difficult to determine.

Why the costume is so popular was a difficult question to answer. Many of us equate it with the ego need to prove how macho one is. It fits right in with the line of thought which equates being a male with power, aggression and violence. So the question still needs to be asked: "Are We Dressing Our Kids to kill?"

We might ask that the next time we put those jungle fatigues in the washing machine, or place them in the child's dresser drawer.

NOW

April 26, 2014

Major retailers in our area, Target, Walmart, and Fred Meyers still stock these clothes in which we dress our kids to kill. I still see the kids and some adults wearing those fatigues. It appears that the video culture is supplanting some of the more militaristic expressions of our culture such as camouflage clothing. It seems to have become the hunting garb color of choice. Add to this the number of mass shootings in recent years. There seems to be no end to our need to assuage the ego with the garb and weapons of violence.

THEN
The Statue of Liberty
July 1, 1986

In speaking of the Statue of Liberty, the designer and builder, Frederic Auguste Bartholdi stated:

"Colossal statuary does not consist simply in making an enormous statue. It ought to produce an emotion in the breast of the spectator, not because of its volume, but because its size is in keeping with the idea that it interprets."

The idea: Democracy.

In the midst of all the hype surrounding the 4th of July and the refurbishing of the Statue of Liberty, the commercializing of the event with gaudy trinkets and silver dollars, with eloquent speeches and quiet moments of reflection; it might we well to remind ourselves of a shift in meaning surrounding the Lady of the Harbor. At the beginning this gift from France was a symbol of friendship and an affirmation of the idea that Democracy was the wave of the future.

This gift of friendship soon became a symbol of new opportunities, of new beginnings, of people seeking a new way of life, of people on the run from economic deprivation and political tyranny. This symbol of friendship became a symbol of immigration.

This emphasis has become immortalized with the words of Emma Lazarus inscribed on the base of the statue.

"Give me your tired, your poor, your huddled masses yearning to breathe free, the wretched refuse of your teeming shore. Send these the homeless, tempest tossed to me. I lift my lamp beside the golden door."

In one sense this invitation to new life reinforced the idea of democracy: openness, freedom, freedom of speech, press, religion and assembly. In response to the invitation issued by the Lady of the Harbor, the immigrants came in the millions: Scots, Germans, Irish, Italians, Slavs, and Jews. These made up the teeming masses yearning to breathe free.

There is Nothing New Under the Sun

But not all Americans have experienced the promise of freedom symbolized by Ms. Liberty. The black American writer, James Baldwin reminds us of the broken and unfulfilled promises offered to black Americans. He writes:

For black Americans, for black inhabitants of this country, the Statue of Liberty is simply a very bitter joke meaning nothing to us.

Perhaps the fact that the Statue symbolizes promises means there is still a possibility of fulfillment, for promises point towards the future.

The light of the Lady's torch needs to illuminate the soul of this nation for it seems to be dark, making a mockery of the promises of liberty. The mood of the land and too many governmental leaders are re-writing the lines of Emma Lazarus.

Send me your skilled, your rich, your professionals, your well educated; send me your ideologically pure, those running from Eastern Europe but not Central America. Send me your deposed tyrants, not those who have and continue to suffer under totalitarian regimes... Send these to me... Keep your teeming masses.

Perhaps the Lady of the Harbor needs to be wrapped in a shroud of mourning. If she could weep she might shed tears as we isolate ourselves from the barefoot immigrants from Central and South America. But there are many who believe in the promises symbolized by Ms. Liberty. As one author has stated:

Perhaps she will become, indeed she has become a new symbol of the struggle against tyranny: one that has nothing to do with taxation without representation or ignorance or poverty, but against the tyranny of the all-powerful state, (I would add the tyranny exercised by us through client states).

Tomorrow she will have another meaning for another generation, for people who set out in rickety ships from Southeast Asia, or who walk north towards the Rio Grande.

These are the ones who find sanctuary in the churches. These are the ones who believe the words of Emma Lazarus.

They believe in LIBERTY.

The Statue of Liberty

This is an idea which cannot be put to death by this administration, or any government in the world.
The idea is as colossal as the Statue of Liberty.
May her torch shine brightly in the years to come.

NOW

2014
Immigration policy of the current Obama administration
Rhetoric of politicians seeking the presidency.
Laws attacking immigrants or profiling Hispanics
Fences along the border

Today's news (5/17/14) brings us one positive note concerning border crossings. The border patrol is establishing centers for the increase in the number of young people fleeing across the border. Also there appears to be not progress on immigration reform in the current political climate. Although the Senate has passed a bill containing a provision for a path to citizenship, it does not stand a chance in the House of Representatives to be passed even though House Majority Leader John Boehner wishes to pass such. I am optimistic about the possibility of such passing in the future for two reasons: the changing demographics (large number of Hispanic voters) and the possible candidacy of Jeb Bush of Florida entering the race. He has a wife of Hispanic descent thus having great appeal to the Hispanic community. Whether Mr. Bush prevails in the field of 11 Republican aspirants remains to be seen. This will be settled subsequent to the publication of this manuscript.
    The current administration has also initiated the "Dream Act" enabling students who came to the United States as children to enter colleges and universities without fear of reprisal and deportation.
    At this writing 7/25/2014 thousands of children are crossing the border from Honduras, Guatemala and El Salvador. In attempting to accommodate them as they are processed by the courts, the administration has sought to relocate them while they

wait for a hearing. Protesters are demonstrating outside shelters in Michigan, Pennsylvania, Texas and California. Some protesters in Michigan are demonstrating with automatic rifles slung over their shoulders. Fear and ignorance are burning brightly in the current political milieu of the presidential campaign of 2014–2016. The rhetoric includes the idea of building a very tall wall across our entire southern border, a constitutional amendment to eliminate the "birthing clause" which grants citizenship to any child born in this country and deporting the estimated 11 million undocumented immigrants. Nativism and xenophobia are alive and thriving in our culture of fear.

Perhaps it is time to erase the words of Emma Lazarus from the Statue of Liberty and inscribe the names of the countries from which people will be welcomed and their ethnic groupings, religious affiliations and technical skills. Above all we need to remove the majestic words of Emma Lazarus from the Lady in the Harbor.

THEN
Violence/The Survival Game
1982

The United States is a violent society. It finds expression on t. v. and in movies, in the increasing popularity of the death penalty, the obscene military buildup at home and around the globe and in our international arms sales.

It has reached such a level of acceptance that it is now a part of the "fun and games" of Americans. Specifically the game which is now making its debut in Northeast Iowa with hardly a whimper of protest is called THE SURVIVAL GAME. You can read about it in the April 18th issue of the *Waterloo Courier*.

If you have not read about it, this is the way it works. The participants divide into two teams. They dress up in camouflage clothing and paint their faces. One gets the impression they are paramilitary units undergoing special training for guerrilla

Violence/The Survival Game

warfare. They are given a weapon, a Nelspot 007 paint gun. These shoot gelatin paintballs, originally designed to mark trees or cattle.

The two teams are turned loose in a sixty acre wooded farmstead in the Waterloo area. Their objective is to capture the flag of the other team and return to home base without being caught or killed. I don't think the teams take prisoners, they are simply killed; that is shot with the gelatin paintballs. When shot the casualty leaves the playing area with his hands in the air.

I reacted to this game, this simulated war game, with great concern. As I explored my reaction I concluded that my response lies in part from its glorification of violence. Violence, simulated violence has become a sport. War, hardly something to be glorified, now becomes "fun and games."

Why do people participate in or endorse this simulated violence? Some reasons given are: "it's a chance to be a kid again," or "get rid of my tensions," or "to add some excitement to my life," and again "to build up my physical condition."

Further reflection on this act of simulated violence speaks to other needs as well. What is it that compels us to endorse so much violence in society at large? What is it that enables us to prepare for and enter into war?

Studies reveal that violence is acceptable because it helps maintain their manliness. In our male dominated society we need wars and the preparation for wars to prove our virility.

But our society is also undergoing change concerning the roles into which men and women, boys and girls have been placed. We are discovering a new man, capable of nurturing and being gentle. Looking at the Survival Game from the perspective of the new man raises questions about the violence in our culture and the males' participation in it. From the perspective of the new man the Survival Game is not acceptable because it leads people into thinking that real war can't be too bad.

Decent folks who get caught up in these games of "simulated violence" should ask themselves questions. Do we really possess an unspoken desire for war itself? Does simulated war prove men's virility?

There is Nothing New Under the Sun

The late Walter Lippmann shared a helpful insight as we think of this equation of the need for war to maintain our virility. He writes:

"If we, even unconsciously, yearn for combat so that we can validate our virility, then we are just like the young German who was overjoyed when World War I broke out.

"I am not ashamed to say" this young man was later to write, "that overwhelmed by impassioned enthusiasm, I fell on my knees and thanked heaven out of my overflowing heart that God had granted me the good fortune of witnessing the Great War." The young man's name was Adolph Hitler.

The thread of civility is being weakened just a little more by the Survival Game. We don't need it.

Gerzon, Mark, A Choice of Heroes, Houghton Mifflin Company, Boston, 1982, page 58.

NOW
The Survival Game
May 17, 2014

As noted earlier this dynamic of violence is being played out in a cascade of video games which keep the youth of our generation "clued" to the computer. Add to that the movies saturated with violence the "survival game" concept is alive and well in our day. The Hunter Game is but one movie predicated on the "survival of the fittest". A final influence is the television. Our culture reeks of violence and at least ten television programs filled with violence are brought to us on a weekly basis. For us on this issue "there is nothing new under the sun."

THEN
America—A Very Religious Nation
December 1983

As 1983 fades into history so do the big stories of the year! Our involvement in the middle east, the truck bombing of the compound of the U.S. Marines, the decline of the rate of inflation, the spiraling of the deficit, the defeat of the ERA in the House, and the invasion of Grenada.

Now I should like to add another story to the list of stories of 1983. It is a story not expressed but certainly reflected in our national behaviour. It is a story which may get even bigger in 1984. That story: The United States is a very religious nation. The people, including the leadership, are a very religious people.

We have a god to which we devote energy, time, resources and life itself. But the god which I saw striding across the nation in the year of 1983 was not the God of the Bible, even though our President declared 1983 to be the "Year of the Bible." The god which commanded our loyalty, one whom we have adored, for whom we have expended much wealth and resources; the god to whom we even made human sacrifices is the god of war: **Mars** is his name in Roman mythology. **Ares** is his Greek counterpart.

Let me tell you about Mars. Originally Mars was a god of farmland and fertility. The month of March was named after him because March was the beginning of the growing season. Mars became the god of war after the Romans came into contact with Greek culture. They gave him many characteristics of the Greek god of war, Ares.

The Greek warriors, in their literature, would run from Ares for he was brutal and violent, delighting in bloody conflict. He was despised by the Greeks. But Mars was loved by the Romans. The warriors would run after him. They would think it "sweet to die in battle" for Mars. Before going into battle Roman troops would offer sacrifices to Mars and after a victory they gave Mars a share of their spoils.

There is Nothing New Under the Sun

1983 was a year when Mars was worshipped with a passion. Motivated by paranoia over our "national security", sacrifices of resources, great amounts of money and flesh and blood human beings were offered to this god as he strode around the globe leaving his footprint in Central America, South Africa, the Middle East, and the Caribbean where he gave to us a sense of importance and righteousness on the island of Grenada.

After those exploits the high priests of industry and the military were rewarded and given a portion of the "spoils" more money, more personnel to keep alive the adoration of the tribal god, Mars.

And the story continues into 1984. Who knows how long this god will remain on the throne of this nation. I see no letup in our adoration of him. But history does remind us there is always a twilight of the gods. H. Richard Niebuhr reminds us of that truth.

"The causes for which we live all die. Social movements do pass and are replaced by others. Ideals we cling to as absolutes are revealed by time to be relative. Empires and cities do decay."[1]

Perhaps all we can hope for is the shackling of Mars for history tells us Mars is always around. The best we can do is to remove him from the stage of history, hoping a more benevolent divine being might dominate our national life. Until then, our nation and others will continue to be very religious nations paying homage to Mars the god of war.

Goodbye 1983. Welcome 1984

NOW
2014/2015

Current efforts to cut the defense budget have met with resistance and those leading are proclaiming their resistance is rooted in the mantra of "interest of national security". Even though they have military bases in their districts they are quick with the disclaimer

---

1. Niebuhr, H. Richard, *Radical Monotheism and Western Culture*, New York, Harper & Brothers, 1943, page 122.

this resistance is not based on the employment the military bases provide in my state. It appears that worship at the altar of Mars continues to be alive and well. The God of Hebrew/Christian scripture with the mandate to care for the marginalized and the vulnerable among us is nowhere to be found in the halls of the budget makers.

We haven't even touched upon the practice of having a "national day of prayer" nor the recent Supreme Court decision defending the opening of public meetings with a prayer, usually offered by Christian clergy and many times referencing Jesus Christ. Alas, we are a "religious nation" indeed.

The recent National Prayer Breakfast was used by the speaker Dr. Carson to denounce the Affordable Care Act. He is also a Republican candidate for the office of the presidency.

Add to that the recent Supreme Court Decision declaring constitutional the opening of council meetings in the upstate New York town of Greece. The "wall" between church and state is being breached once again.

THEN

Geraldine Ferraro

Another First/Not the Last

July 20, 1984

A few years ago the United Nations passed a resolution naming 1975 as the International Year of the Women.

The year 1984 will surely be considered the year of the political woman in the United States. Geraldine Ferraro has made it so, not only for the Democrats but for people of all political persuasions.

In these days following the convention of Democrats in San Francisco, everyone is talking about Geraldine Ferraro. Projections are being made about the influence Representative Ferraro will have on the '84 elections. As I reflect on the convention, without a

There is Nothing New Under the Sun

doubt the highlight of the convention was the acceptance speech by Mrs. Ferraro.

What captured my attention and impressed me most were the response registered on the on the faces of the women in the hall. The cameras caught the feelings of so many, the looks on their faces, the tears running down their cheeks. These faces told me that Ferraro's presence was therapeutic, almost cathartic. Relief, emotional fatigue, elation, something almost mystical was happening. It was as though the frustrations experienced by women over the decades—no centuries, were released. They were experiencing great satisfaction over the completion of a long, tedious race; the race for equality in the political process.

If one were to believe in the spirit of political past, one could feel the presence of Susan B. Anthony and other suffragettes of sixty, seventy or eighty years ago. Representative Ferraro's mother symbolized for me this movement from the past. The phrase by Jesse Jackson seems so apt: "The time of the politically attuned women had come…"

The women were celebrating the fact that the very foundations of political party sexism had been shaken. The question remains: will the electorate's sexism have its foundations shaken as profoundly? Will she be evaluated on the substantive issues and not the issue of gender?

Posing the question tells us how far we have to go. Electorate sexism will not be put to rest until that observation is no longer considered. More happened at this convention than the opening of the door to a particular office. The historical movement for women's suffrage has reached a new level of participation. Win or lose 51% of the population now has an articulate representative and advocate at the highest level of American political dialogue.

Representative Geraldine Ferraro is the first woman carrying the battle for equality to the threshold of the office of the vice president and she will not only have to cope with the ordinary expectations laid on all political candidates, but the unrealistic ones which go with being *the first* nominee of the two major political parties.

The Recovery of Imagination

NOW
Candidacy of Hillary Clinton
April 24, 2015

Although Geraldine Ferraro was the first woman nominated by one of the two major political parties, she was not the first woman to have her name placed in nomination for the presidency. Back in 1872 Victoria Woodhull was on the ballot of The Equal Rights Party, Belma Ann Lockwood was a vice presidential candidate of the Equal Rights Party. In 1884 Mary Etta Stow was a vice presidential candidate on the ticket of the Equal Rights Party. Historically there were women on the tickets of the Green Party and the Communist Party. Angela Davis ran on the ticket and was able to glean 3.7 million votes.

If the current political trend can be trusted it appears that Hillary Clinton could well become the next Democratic Candidate for the Presidency. She announced her candidacy formally on April 18, 2015. Perhaps Elizabeth Warren, the Senator from Massachusetts could be her vice presidential running mate. The Republican Party has a woman seeking the nomination: Carly Fiorina. Finally, women are claiming their voices in spite of male resistance to those voices.

THEN
The Recovery of Imagination
January 4, 1984

"It is better to light a candle than to curse the darkness."

For months I have been lamenting the absence of imagination on the political scene. I've noted this absence in the office of the President and in the actions and rhetoric of the 8 Democrats seeking the office of the presidency.

But now along comes Jesse Jackson with his trip to Syria. He participated in a face to face conversation with President Assad. On humanitarian grounds he appeals to Assad for the release of Lt.

There is Nothing New Under the Sun

Robert Goodman, Jr. After several days of negotiations Goodman is released.

The candle of imaginative action has been lit illuminating the darkness of the Middle East morass. A bit of light has been shed in the tunnel of our involvement in Lebanon.

The political writers have begun to sharpen their pens as they did prior to this journey. "What were Jackson's motives? What impact will his trip have on his candidacy? How will it impact the other aspirants in the camp of the Democrats? Will there be any change in the administration's policy in the Middle East?"

George Will repeated what he had said earlier: "This is a most improper way to conduct foreign policy. It is illegal. Jackson exploited a situation and was exploited by the Syrians!"

People have been calling in to radio talk shows praising and criticizing Jackson. A comment by one critical of Jackson caught my attention. He stated: "We don't resolve problems that way!"

That is the point of all this. The candle in the darkness of our Mideast involvement was an act of a live imagination, not that of tired, bureaucratic haggling. The commodity of imagination is scarce in governmental circles. The same old way of doing diplomacy has fostered nothing but great anxiety at home and around the world.

Imagine what might happen to the international climate if our President tried something imaginative, like saying something complimentary about the Soviets, or if they said something nice about us? How exciting it would be if our President made a trip to Moscow or even inquired, publicly about the health of Mr. Andropov?

The world is getting weary of being held hostage by the mutual threats of the superpowers. The time has come for some imaginative action to break the impasse of suspicion and hostility.

We may need one voice speaking in an official capacity for the United States but if that official voice is muted or lacking in imagination, perhaps citizen diplomacy might be necessary to shift public opinion.

Can the children of Isaac & Ishmael live in peace?

Imagination is a desperately needed gift in these dangerous times. It might illuminate the darkness created by fear, pride and the arrogance of power dominating the global scene.

The candle of the Jackson journey, however short-lived that candle might be, has made an impact far greater than the immediate end achieved.

President Reagan said, "All America thanks you, Mr. Jackson." Now, Mr. President, go and light some more candles.

NOW
The release of Sgt. Bowe Bergdahl
June 14, 2014

The negotiations surrounding the release of Sgt. Bergdahl took five years to bring his release about. There is much political rhetoric being spread across the land besmirching Bergdahl's character and the fact that President Obama facilitated the release of prisoners into the Taliban's hands. The last word is yet to be spoken on Sgt. Bowe Bergdahl. New information has come to light surrounding Sgt. Bergdahl's departure from his post. The end result of the investigating not

with standing imaginative overtures to foster the release of hostages is always welcomed. Perhaps candle lighting in 2014/2015 can be seen in a new role for the military as it participated in the Ebola epidemic and the earthquakes and floods in the Philippines, Japan and Nepal.

THEN
Can the children of Isaac & Ishmael live in peace?
September 20, 1982

Menachem Begin rejects President Reagan's Mideast peace initiative with the words "... Samaria and Judea belong to Israel forever." He uses biblical names for the territory called the West Bank. On

There is Nothing New Under the Sun

the other side, Yasser Arafat in his letter to Pope John Paul asks for justice for "... the other children of Abraham."

In coffee shops on Atlantic Avenue in the Palestinian section of New York City, Palestinians speak of not wanting their children to become captive to the American culture for they are waiting to return to their homeland.

Both Jews and Palestinians make a claim upon and have passionate love for the same land. The cause for this claim and not love goes beyond and overwhelms the political realities. The cause is a religious one fueled by the religious question; "to whom was the land promised?"

As we answer this question we discover that both the children of Isaac and Ishmael have much in common which could be the basis for dialogue.

As we look at their lineage we see the Jews tracing their heritage to Abraham, to Abraham, Sarah and Isaac. The Palestinians trace theirs to Abraham, Hagar and Ishmael.

In the Genesis Record both warring brothers were promised nationhood by God.

Both have a legitimate claim upon the land called Palestine prior to the United Nations' mandate to establish two states.

Both have experienced exile. For the Jews it has been ages long from the year 90.

And for the Palestinians since 1948. The Jews have been persecuted and ghettoized through the centuries. I remember walking in the old town of Prague, Czechoslovakia where the Jewish community is located. In centuries past this was the walled ghetto of their community. They were unable to buy land outside the ghetto or bury their dead beyond the walls. The cemeteries are layered with graves and gravestones are clustered together. The Palestinians are being ghettoized by the Israeli government most blatantly by the settlement programs, the latest being carried out on the West Bank.

Their common love for the land is obvious to everyone except each other. Both are chained to the past. It shapes their policies. The day seems to be a long way off before the demands for peace

Can the children of Isaac & Ishmael live in peace?

becomes greater than the fears and insecurities seared into the souls of both by the past.

Movement toward peace will not take place until the Israeli and Palestinians recognize each other's claims and remember their common experiences. Both have a common lineage, experiences of exile, persecution and being ghettoized, living scattered throughout the world without a homeland, and a passionate longing for a homeland.

Awareness of their similar histories might free them from their bondage to the past which produces so much death in the present. It might enable them to see the other's point of view and create a new vision for the holy land.

NOW
Visit to the Holy Lands
Pope Francis
May 24, 25, 2014

The visit of Pope Francis to the Holy Lands injected a new possibility into the moribund peace process. He was welcomed as a head of state by the Israelis and by the Palestinian authorities. His visit was viewed a one head of state, the Vatican, visiting heads of state, the Palestinian Leader Abbas and the Israeli leader Shimon Peres. The most promising and moving part of those encounters was the extension of an invitation by His Holiness to both men to "come to my house" and join me in prayer. Both accepted. Perhaps the promise of a two state solution to this historic impasse might finally happen. Most certainly it will be nudged along a little bit. Perhaps the children of Isaac and the children of Ishmael will be able to live in peace. However, as of this writing some of the Sons of Ishmael, namely Hamas is engaged in rocket warfare and missile exchanges, with Israel. The people of Gaza are suffering horribly and Israel is experiencing losses as well. Tunnels used by Hamas to infiltrate Israel are being destroyed. The cycle of violence continues as it has for decades if not generations.

There is Nothing New Under the Sun

Events in the Holy Lands are outrunning the content of this commentary. In recent days Prime Minister Netanyahu gave mixed signals concerning a two state solution to the crisis. Currently relations between him and President Obama are strained. They have become more so with President Obama's pursuit of a nuclear test ban treaty with Iran.

THEN
Cynicism
1984

In the 4th century B. C. E. a man named Diogenes walked the streets of Athens in broad daylight with a lantern. He was looking for an honest man.

On another occasion he entered a theatre when everyone else was leaving it.

Unable to secure housing in Athens, he chose to live in a tub.

These eccentric actions by Diogenes were symbols of a philosophical system which advocated the rights of the individual in the extreme; that system: cynicism.

The intention of the cynic was to expose the artificiality of convention, of society's customs. They wanted to free persons from bondage to all custom, convention or institution, by reducing our desires to the basics. They renounced all others imposed by civilization.

Their primary tools were outspokenness and shamelessness in action. They used these tools to expose the pretensions of "intellectuals" and politicians.

They were so indifferent to the conventions of society and such ardent missionaries of "doing what is natural" they encouraged people to go barefoot, eat and make love in public, sleep in tubs or at the crossroads of the community. They believed that shamelessness was superior to modesty.

From those origins we move quickly to the popular understanding of cynicism in our time. To people today it means an

Cynicism

attitude of position which questions the sincerity and goodness of people's motives and actions. Cynics today hold a contemptuous disbelief in human goodness and sincerity, not just question it.

Unfortunately there seems to be considerable evidence to support the cynic's case.

In recent days two cities in Illinois were campaigning to have the state build a new prison in their community, when a couple of years ago they were against it. It seems the reasons for not building it were no longer valid in the light of economic survival. One might become cynical about such matters and suggest the eloquent principles inevitably take second place to the god of money. Ah, but who can blame them. Cynically speaking, maybe everything does filter down to economics and self-interest.

In the realm of sports, USC has been disciplined by the NCAA for permitting its football coach to sell at inflated prices tickets given to the athletes and turning the profits over to the athletes. When questioned about it USC students simply commented cynically, "everyone does it!" Why the display (pretentious display) of virtue?

What is true in the chambers of commerce in the towns of Illinois and on the campuses of the land is present in the political realm and in business. For example, the utility companies speak of serving us as they raise prices and even persuade Congress to compel the consumer to assist the company in the building of a gas line from Alaska. Serving?

The pretentious behavior is not only reserved for those in the field of athletics, politics and business. It is present in the field of religion and the church, and among academics and academia. Speaking of academics, I was visiting with a friend the other day who is in the employ of UNI and told him about Diogenes walking the streets of Athens with his lantern in broad daylight looking for an honest man. In response he stated at the University of Northern Iowa someone stole the lantern.

Who can be surprised by the mood of cynicism prevalent in the land? You know, there could be something healthy in the ghost of Diogenes walking among us puncturing our pretence of virtue.

There is Nothing New Under the Sun

Perhaps his lantern will illuminate the presence of honest women and men among us!

NOW
Cynicism
August 16, 2015

If there is anything today (July 27, 2015) that speaks to the reality of cynicism it is the general climate surrounding the political campaign for the office of the Presidency of the United States. This is particularly true in the group of individuals (17 to date) running for the Republican nomination. More and more the rhetoric is becoming more volatile. Today (July 27, 2015) we heard former Governor Mike Huckabee accusing Obama of "marching the Israelis to the door of the oven." This is a reference to the holocaust to be sure… This is zenith of cynicism. The Republican debate on August 6, 2015 saw a major display of cynicism in the rhetoric of the candidates in the manner in which they framed the positions of their opponents and the Obama administration. It is as though they were running from reason.

THEN

Auschwitz, the Holocaust and Remembering
February 1, 1985

The week of January 27th saw the 40th Anniversary of the liberation of the death camp at Auschwitz by the Russians. At that place 4 million men, women and children died, most of whom if not all were Jews. Elie Wiesel, the novelist who survived Auschwitz called it "The Place of Eternal Night…"

To speak of Auschwitz and the Holocaust, one must speak softly lest one violate the dead and injure the memories of the living by ill-chosen words.

I speak to identify a thread, a characteristic which runs through the fabric of human history, a thread which became

Auschwitz, the Holocaust and Remembering

bonds holding together the crusade against the Jews. It is a thread, a dimension of our character to which we all might cling if we are not alert.

That thread is the need for a scapegoat.

The need to blame someone for my behavior,

The need to blame someone for the ills of the times, someone who could be the recipient of our frustrations, our hostilities, someone to blame in order to do what we want to do, to justify tragic behavior.

The Jews became the scapegoat fueling the Nazi ambitions to conquer Europe.

In history scapegoating has had an honorable ritualistic purpose. In ancient Jerusalem the scapegoat was one of two goats received by the Jewish High Priest. The priest would lay his hands on the scapegoat as he confessed the sins of the people. Then he would send the goat into the wilderness. This symbolized the idea that their sins had been put away or forgiven.

Today the scapegoat has taken on more a more insidious meaning. It is applied to another person, or a people in the case of the Jews in the Third Reich. That person or people are made to take the blame for something which is the fault of another.

The Jewish people became the scapegoat of the Nazi ideology. They were offered up on the altars of religion and nationalism. How else might we explain Christians manning the gas chambers and the ovens? How else would we explain the alliance of the Axis: Germany, the birthplace of Martin Luther's Reformation, and Italy the heart of the Catholic Church? In these countries people regularly went to church every Sunday. What a frightening irony!

Could the holocaust or at least persecution in a more sophisticated version happen in this country? To apply that possibility to any group of people in this country would require a monumental leap from Auschwitz. To do so might violate the sanctity of the 4,000,000 who died there.

But I wonder...

As frustration mounts in the hearts of so many people over their economic plight, as this administration continues to experience frustration over its inability to wield its will abroad with total impunity, without creating an outcry from allies and at home; I wonder where the scapegoat might surface and persecution follow?

Auschwitz and the Holocaust can save the human race if we remember!

In his forward to the book "Voices from the Holocaust", Elie Wiesel implores us to listen to the voices. What they have to say about their past constitutes the basis for our future.

> "Fanaticism leads to racism,
> Racism leads to hate,
> Hate leads to murder,
> murder to the death of the species.
> The danger lies in forgetting.
> Forgetting however, will not affect only the dead.
> Should it triumph, the ashes of yesterday will cover
> our hopes for tomorrow. (page 4)

If the scapegoat mentality gets loose in the land, the observations made by Rabbi Seymour Siegel, Director of the Holocaust Memorial Council could well be confirmed for it would be consistent with the facts of history.

"The human heart is evil above all things!"

The scapegoat needs to be sent only into the wilderness of Sinai, not into other people or nations.

NOW

Scapegoating
August 16, 2014

The practice of scapegoating did not end with the holocaust as we well know. We have seen it practiced several years ago when the auto industry was having great difficulty. Workers in Detroit were photographed beating a Japanese car with bats to vent their rage, their frustration. The Japanese were the scapegoats at that moment.

As women sought their legitimate place in industry and board room, they were considered to be the cause of economic difficulties at the time.

Now the primary scapegoat for our economic difficulties has been immigrant workers, documented and undocumented. Recipients of the benefits of our safety net have become scapegoats for some. The consequences of scapegoating the immigrant have been felt in the agricultural sector with the ruining of crops in California and Georgia to name a few.

As the legalization of same-sex marriage becomes prevalent in the land our gay and lesbians are blamed in some quarters for the breakdown of marriages in the

heterosexual community. To understand the factors informing societal ills including the economic difficulties taking place on a global level requires making the effort to become informed. Alas, the necessary required thinking and discernment takes effort and time. These qualities are pushed aside for quick answers to complex problems. Therefore one has to be vigilant to be aware of the scapegoat moving about in the "thicket of our culture". We need to be alert as to which group will become the scapegoat du jour.

THEN
Martin Niemoeller
April 17, 1984

> "When the Nazis came to get the communist,
> I was silent.
> When they came to get the socialists,
> I was silent.
> When they came to get the Catholics,
> I was silent.
> When they came to get the Jews,
> I was silent.
> And when they came to get me,
> There was no one left to speak." (Martin Niemoeller)

There is Nothing New Under the Sun

On March 6th of this year the man who spoke those words died. His name: Martin Niemoeller. Although his death was noted in the religious press and editorially in the *Des Moines Register* of March 11th, another glance at this man is in order as he leaves the stage of History. His life and actions serve as a model of courage for all who might become weary in the struggle for peace and justice in our time.

Although he died a Lutheran Pastor, he began his adult life as a German U-boat commander in World War I. He was a militant patriot and a leader in the Academic Defense Corps, an armed student nationalist organization which he helped create.

In his maturing years as a Lutheran pastor he found himself on a collision course with the Third Reich. During the rise of Hitler the church became controlled by Nazis sympathizers. An edict was issued calling for the removal of all pastors with Jewish origins. In response to that Niemoeller organized the Pastor's Emergency League. They pooled their resources, spiritual and material to support the dismissed pastors.

By September 1933 there was a widespread response to this call for help and almost overnight Niemoeller became the key spokesman for the German churches opposition to Hitler.

This "Pastor's Emergency League" became the main force in creating what became known as the Confessing Church. Its theology was one of the cross and not Germanic superiority. One of its failures, in spite of its courageous witness was this; it did not oppose Hitler or the Nazi state in the political realm. He confessed this failure on the part of the church. It was that failure which brought forth the condemnation of the silent ones in the face of tyranny.

The opposition to the Nazi regime did bring the Confessing Church under attack. By the summer of 1939 most of its members were removed from the scene through imprisonment or the draft. In 1937 Niemoeller was arrested and imprisoned in Berlin and finally in Dachau. He spent eight years in prison for his opposition to Hitler.

Martin Niemoeller

Following the war Niemoeller became a leader in the post war church. He called the attention of the churches to the dangers of self-interest, its own survival if that concern is muting its message of freedom, peace and justice in the face of oppression. His voice was a minority voice in opposition to the rearming of Germany. He became president of the German Peace Society. In 1967 he visited Hanoi where he criticized the U. S. role in Vietnam. In his role as peacemaker he marched in Hamburg a few years ago with more than 700,000 people protesting the nuclear arms race.

He was an architect of the ecumenical movement and a leader in the creation of and a president of the World Council of Churches.

Because of his sense of failure on the part of the church to speak out against the rise of the tyrannical Third Reich, Niemoeller calls all of us to be aware of the trap into which the church might fall; namely becoming the handmaid of the state. Conversely he would challenge those who would make the state the handmaid of a particular brand of religion. In these troubled times, let us remember the message of Martin Niemoeller. For in our day there are many who want to create a marriage between church and state which can only be destructive to both parties.

NOW
Silence is the Voice of Complicity
May 31, 2014

If there is one truth every pastor needs to post on the wall of his/her study it is that statement: "Silence is the Voice of Complicity". Next to it one could place his insightful verses about silence.

> "When the Nazis came to get the Communists
> I was silent.
> When they came to get the Socialists,
> I was silent.
> When they came to get the Catholics,
> I was silent.
> When they came to get the Jews,

There is Nothing New Under the Sun

> I was silent.
> And when they came to get me,
> There was no one left to speak."

Hitler had his theologians: Gerhard Kittel, Paul Althaus, and Emanuel Hirsch. Let us not lose our integrity or our voice to be a critic of the social order, particularly when it comes to war. Since WW II we have seen the silence of too many clergy and laypeople during the Vietnam War, and subsequently current wars, Iraq and Afghanistan. We haven't even begun to address the silence of the churches with regard to our involvement in the "dirty wars" in Nicaragua or El Salvador. Because of the war in El Salvador we are haunted by the ghost of Archbishop Oscar Romero. He was assassinated on March 24, 1980, while celebrating mass in the hospital chapel. I visited that chapel in 1986. It was a poignant moment for me.

THEN
Intolerance
April 3, 1984

On April 3rd Governor Terry Branstad hosted the annual "Governor's Prayer on Breakfast." The Governor invited several Rabbis to the event and they respectfully chose not to attend. They surmised, correctly, the event would be exclusively Christian in nature. They would have been subjected to Christian testimonials. Forgetting that he is the Governor of all Iowans, including members of the Jewish community, and others, Branstad reacted defensively and insensitively,

He said: "It (the event) has been that way, exclusively Christian, for 25 years. I am sensitive to their feelings. But it has been basically a Christian event in this state and other states and I don't object to that." That display of intolerance could easily have been avoided if he had simply chosen not to invite the Rabbis and bill the event as a breakfast only for clergy of the Christian persuasion.

Intolerance

But the season of intolerance and insensitivity will not end with the Governor's prayer breakfast. It will be perpetuated in countless high school auditoriums throughout the state as once again we have Christian clergy pronouncing invocations and benedictions at commencement exercises.

How long will it take for people of the Christian tradition to realize that there are people of other religious persuasions living in their communities?

How long will it take people to sense there may be a violation of the first amendment to the Constitution which prohibits using the state as an instrument for religious indoctrination?

How long will it take for the clergy, who should know better, to cease bowing to the god of civil religion and making their invocations and benedictions so vague as to be acceptable that they say nothing and violate the integrity of their own traditions?

Or, on the other side, how long will it take for the clergy to realize they cannot make their invocations and benedictions too specific in order to maintain their integrity without being guilty of imposing their religious beliefs on non-Christians or even non-believers who claim no religious traditions?

The intolerance and insensitivity to the majority this time of the year is frightening and divisive. For this intolerance and insensitivity to cease lawsuits have to be initiated. This is what happened in the U. S. District Court for the Southern District of Iowa last May 9th.

The Central Community School District of Decatur County had an injunction issued against it which prohibited a Christian pastor from giving an invocation and benediction at a commencement exercise scheduled for May 12, 1985.

It is unfortunate, but not surprising, that the civil courts have to call some Christians to accountability in their efforts to proselytize under the umbrella of a state sponsored and supported event.

When this happens the religious traditions involved are the better for it. They are called to claim their own identity independent of the need to appease all involved by some vague, innocuous

47

There is Nothing New Under the Sun

expression of piety. And they are called to a new level of tolerance and respect for the religious traditions of others.

Are more lawsuits necessary to attain these benefits?

When will this season of intolerance come to its well-deserved demise?

NOW
Intolerance Today
June 17, 2014/August 11, 2015

Note resistance to Muslims rebuilding a community center near the sight of the twin towers tragedy? Recall the resistance to building a mosque in Murfreesboro, Tenn. Make note of other acts of intolerance, violence against persons of other faith traditions. Intolerance found expression in North Carolina when three Muslim students were killed. Allegedly the killing was over a parking spot. According to the New York Times (3/4/15) it is being viewed as a hate crime. The prosecutor plans to seek the death penalty. Finally we have an expression of intolerance fed by religious sentiment in the community of Troutdale, Oregon. There a young member of the LDS faith community went on a shooting spree to kill "sinners". What is needed is a replaying of South Pacific's song: "you've got to be carefully taught to love and hate."

Intolerance finds expression in the absolutist position of religious fundamentalist and those who cling to dogma in the Roman Catholic Church in the light of changing cultural mores. It is frightening when individuals believe they are "speaking for God."

Intolerance has a global reach. In Sri Lanka today Buddhist monks and lay organizations repeatedly attack minority communities, including Christians. According to Philip Jenkins writing in the August 5, 2015 issue of Christian Century. The Sangha order of Buddhist monks are enforcers of purity against all outsiders. In Myanmar Buddhist clergy are considered super patriotic vigilantes.

The world is keenly aware of the Muslims seeking to establish a caliphate across the middle east. Intolerance is thriving across much of the world. Dr. Jenkins makes note of Hindus and Muslims attacking each other. To understand the need for a reformation within the Muslim Tradition I refer the reader to *Heretic: Why Islam Needs a Reformation Now* by Ayaan Hirsi Ali.

THEN
Violence and Guns,
Or
The Lone Ranger needs to go,
Or
The World at High Noon
January 14, 1983

"Out of the past comes the thundering hoof beats of the great horse Silver. The Lone Ranger rides again."

In my youth these familiar words and music (William Tell Overture), would find me listening intently to the radio as the centuries old battle of good and evil was carried out in my imagination. The "good guys" would triumph over the "bad guys" in the fight for justice.

What I experienced for that half hour was frontier justice. It spoke of a time proven and accepted of dealing with conflict: VIOLENCE!

It even gave to the world a definition of manhood: carry a gun on your hip (two if you can afford them) and a rifle in the saddle scabbard. Although the Lone Ranger has ridden off into the sunset, the spirit of the frontier and violence is still very much with us.

Violence is rampant on the global scene as well as the personal. It is as though the entire world is acting out some drama at "High Noon". From one end of main street come the "good guys". From the other end come the "bad guys".

There is Nothing New Under the Sun

The superpowers set the pace as they square off with their holsters full of nuclear weapons. The rest of us line up in our homes and communities with an arsenal of violent attitudes, words, economic weapons and physical violence.

One key component in this atmosphere of violence is the presence of The American Pet: the Gun.

Happiness is a warm gun.

The frontier mentality of the Lone Ranger episodes and the High Noon movie finds expression in the possession of long guns and handguns. The long gun has found an ignoble use in Waterloo in recent days with the killing of a Waterloo attorney.

Handguns have been used in numerous robberies in the area. They are also used to settle domestic quarrels. Even children use them to kill each other (accidentally of course with guns presumed to be unloaded).

Guns are used to shoot at and sometimes kill presidents, senators, leaders of various groups: George Lincoln Rockwell of the American Nazi Party and Dr. Martin Luther King, Jr. the great civil/human rights leader. We must not forget the children. This household pet aimed at keeping out would be burglar is 5 times more apt to harm a family member than an intruder. According to the National Council for a Responsible Firearms Policy, since the killing of President John F. Kennedy on November 22, 1963, more than 440,000 Americans have been killed by firearms in this country. Over 1.7 million more were wounded by gunfire and approximately 2.7 million were robbed at gunpoint.

There are at least 150 million guns in this country. Of that number some 50–60 million are handguns.

Blame for the violence of the times is placed on everyone's doorsteps but one's own: the schools, television, the breakdown of discipline in the home, the church because they are not teaching respect for authority, the feminist movement taking women out of the home, the gay community because they blur the lines of role expectations and traditional views of men and women, the refugees who have tried to find a new life in this land. These kinds of charges are just scapegoating.

The conditions are many which place people on a collision course with one another on Main Street at High Noon. But one place to begin to lower the level of violence is most certainly tightening the control of the possession of long guns and handguns. Registration of guns is a good beginning, banning the possession of handguns is a better place.

Perhaps the mentality of the frontier can be changed if all the bullets are turned in, not just one "silver bullet" left behind as the Lone Ranger makes his exit.

We could all breathe a deep sigh of relief and get off Main Street when the Lone Ranger and the frontier mentality symbolized by those stories would say

"Hi, ho Silver, away…" for good.

NOW
School Massacres
Congressional Budget
CDC research
April 24, 2015

To speak of guns today calls to mind immediately the school massacres from Columbine in Colorado to Newtown, Ct. And yet in spite of those and other massacres (and that is the appropriate word) we are unable to bring about gun control even at the unthreatening place of background checks. The National Rifle Association is the primary agency spreading fear in the lands about the deprivation of the individual's right to own guns. They lean on the 2nd Amendment to the Constitution, "A well-regulated Militia, being necessary to the security of a Free State, the right of the people to keep and bear Arms, shall not be infringed." The hands of the NRA are saturated with the blood of the innocent.

There is Nothing New Under the Sun

The Congressional Budget
The CDC

In the 2014 Budget proposed by the House of Representatives, Representative Kingston of Georgia stated there will not be the $10,000,000 requested by the Center for Disease Control to do research on the matrix of gun violence in our culture.

The idea of controlling firearms has been frozen and mummified. The killing of children at Columbine and Newtown has not been able to change the mindset of gun advocates and their interpretation of the 2nd Amendment which focused on a well-organized militia. It is becoming common place to have states in which one can "open carry" a firearm including rifles. The country seems to be building a new scenario for High Noon. Main Street is being created. The clock is moving to yet another high noon. Only this time there is a person with a gun and at the other end are the innocent children in classrooms, unsuspecting youth on college campuses, theatre goers sitting in a darkened theatre. The culture of violence in our country which endorses a gun in every pocket is so deeply entrenched no amount of children being killed, presidents and senators being assassinated, bystanders victimized by gang warfare; not even this cascade of death by the gun will make a difference in the mindset of those individuals in the NRA and other pro-gun lobbies who are comfortable with mayhem even at the expense of common sense. The gun culture is built on fear. It is a threat to democracy.

In the current campaign for the presidency (2016) the Republican candidates are making a pilgrimage to the NRA convention in Memphis, Tennessee reinforcing their bona fide as NRA staunch supporters. Remembering that the NRA and their supporters oppose even the most innocuous regulations relative to guns; it seems ironic that as the conventioneers entered the hall with its acres of guns, they had to remove the firing pins of any guns they might have been carrying. I wonder what happened to the idea of a 2nd amendment infringement.

Smile and say Cheese

In the light of the federal government's paralysis in legislating sensible control measures being captive to the NRA mass killings continue. Emmanuel African Methodist Episcopal Church in Charleston, South Carolina has been a most recent venue: June 17, 2015. Nine church folks shot and killed by a man they invited to their prayer meeting. An historic moment came when as the result of a video of the shooter wrapped in a Confederate Battle Flag, the flags of the Confederacy are being removed from state houses across the region. Because it has always been a flag devoted to a wrong; the bondage of a people, African Americans by white "masters", merchandise and flags bearing that symbol are being removed from store shelves of major chains and from license plates.

At the Funeral service for Dr. Pinkney, President Barak Obama gave one of the greatest speeches of any President; the Eulogy for the senior pastor of Emmanuel A.M. E. Dr. Clementa Pinkney. Some historians have placed it along side of Lincoln's Second Inaugural in its significance and eloquence. I doubt if anyone in this country will soon forget the poignant closing of that eulogy: President Barak Obama spontaneously singing Amazing Grace and the congregation joining in.

THEN
Smile and say Cheese
November 12, 1982

"Smile and say cheese."

This is a phrase which takes on new meaning in these days of "cheesy lines". It has become more than an attention getter for having our pictures taken. I am choosing to speak it as a slogan identifying the cruel attempt on the part of the administration to placate the hungry in the land whose numbers are increasing dramatically from week to week. I hear it as an invitation to participate in an act of "hypocritical charity" not unlike the ancient attempt to keep the masses happy by giving them "bread and circuses".

There is Nothing New Under the Sun

This line signifies a political issue: the economic policies of the administration which fail to provide adequate food programs for the needy citizenry, the failure of the administration to provide jobs which enable people to purchase "cheese" and smile the smiles of human dignity.

This phrase points to the administration's effort to shore up the wealth of one group, namely the dairy industry whose entrepreneurs can really "smile and say cheese" and diminish the assets and destroy the dignity of those who stand in line.

Smile and say cheese calls our attention to the destruction of human dignity as TV cameras show us the anger, embarrassment and sadness etched on the faces of those who stand in line. This phrase reminds us of those who are subsidized by our government. The dairy industry in 1981 received $2 billion to enhance the income of about 216,000 commercial dairy producers. The Department of Agriculture bought and stored 350 million pounds of butter, 575 million pounds of cheese and 850 million pounds of dry milk. (AWAS newsletter, p. 4, October 1982)

As I think about that subsidy and the lines of recipients of those products I begin to wonder if the cynics really are correct when they say, "if the Reaganauts didn't have the poor and hungry they would have to invent poverty to deal with the surplus."

In the light of what many of us perceive to be "hypocritical charity" questions must be raised about the administration's priorities. More cuts are anticipated in food and nutrition programs. The Pentagon's appetite will continue to be satiated. The administration will continue to resist creating jobs programs. Government will continue to cease to be the government of all the people.

"Smile and say cheese" should be a phrase reserved for the taking of pictures and not for TV cameras recording the desperate plight of the unemployed, although there could be a sensitizing feature in recording tragedy.

THEN
Patriotism
July 5, 1985

Samuel Johnson, the 18th Century English critic, author and conversationalist Observed: "Patriotism is the last refuge of a scoundrel." One could debate with Johnson as to whether patriotism might be the first refuge of the scoundrel instead of the last. But the fact is that it is too often a refuge for scoundrels or unscrupulous individuals and organizations including government. On that we would agree.

It seems appropriate that as the sounds of fireworks, speeches about the greatness of this country, the singing of songs which touch the heartstrings, and the sounds of marching bands fade into the background, and as Hollywood celebrities like Ann Margret board their planes to fly back to the west coast: it seems appropriate that we take a look at this issue of PATRIOTISM. These are times when loyalty to our government's programs and policies is being equated with patriotism.

Indeed, with President Reagan leading the parade we are being immersed in a sea of red, white and blue rhetoric and symbols. Remember the convention halls at both the Republican and Democrat meetings last fall. We observed a phenomenal display of red, white and blue bunting as well as flags too numerous to count. And who can forget the uproar which followed the actions of one American Legion Post which issued a statement opposing our policies in Central America. What about the debate surrounding the funding of the Contras seeking to overthrow the Nicaraguan government or that surrounding the MX? The issue: Patriotism, meaning the bottom line, loyalty to one's country. The problem lies in the manner in which that loyalty is expressed. As noted in the popular mind and in the heart and mind of President Reagan, it means almost literally; lockstep obedience to this administration's policies. Certainly this is a distorted view of patriotism. However, it is not the first time patriotism has been exaggerated or distorted. In World War I the loyalty of Americans of German ancestry was

There is Nothing New Under the Sun

questioned. In that era even the churches fell victim to this need to prove their loyalty. Placing the American Flag in the sanctuary became the badge of loyalty. In World War II, thousands of patriotic Japanese Americans were placed in detentions camps because of unreasonable fears. Since World War II, some states have tried to make the signing of special oaths a requirement for the job.

But there are others who believe that a higher form of patriotism is found in the opposing of government policies and actions when these are considered unjust and unwise.

We have an admirable history to draw on. One can quickly call to mine Henry David Thoreau who spent time in jail for refusing to pay taxes to support the Mexican-American War. From that experience his influential essay came:

"Civil Disobedience."

In recent history those who resisted the rise of Hitler and Nazism we consider patriots because in their resistance they expressed a profound love of country.

Those who resist government policies today and shelter refugees, refuse to pay a portion of their taxes or declare themselves conscientious objector: might they be patriots too? History will write the verdict on these dissenters in our time. In the meantime waving the flag, and belonging to certain groups, and uncritically following the policies of this administration does not a patriot make.

These actions could well be the behavior of scoundrels seeking refuge from the hard light of critical analysis.

NOW
Patriotism
July 25, 2015

Patriotism appears to be a quieter presence in 2015. There is no draft now that we have a volunteer army. There continues to be some protest over our continued involvement in Iraq and Afghanistan, but the military is now playing a role in aiding victims of natural disasters and outbreaks of epidemics such as Ebola. These expressions of our military's involvement are such to make our country proud of our armed services.

The public expressions of patriotism experience on the National Mall this July 4th has been one of modest reminder of our military presence in our national life. It is a fitting tribute to our historical struggles against tyranny in its myriad manifestations.

THEN
Fear
October 9, 1985

Franklin Delano Roosevelt, in a time of unparalleled difficulty told the people of the United States in his radio address: "We have nothing to fear but fear itself." Good advice then and good advice now.

Although the feeling of fear can be a positive motivating force for the ordering of life and society, the fear permeating our society today has built within it the possibility for the rise of authoritarian forms of governmental behavior, for the subverting of individual liberties, for class and racial hatred; indeed for persecution of a religious and non-religious persons such as humanists.

Fear is the driving force behind the arms race. It is the scourge behind our policies in Central America, translation: the Communist threat. Fear motivates people to bring back the death penalty. It feeds the resistance to handgun control. It makes people willing to give up their basic civil rights for a "porridge of perceived security."

Fear among the citizens enables Ed Meese to push for a change in the Supreme Court's Miranda Decision which requires arresting officers to tell you and me of our right to legal counsel. Fear is that reality which prevents white males from sharing power, economic and political with women and minorities.

Fear of economic collapse on the part of farmers and others is swelling the ranks of hate-mongering groups such as the Christian

There is Nothing New Under the Sun

Patriots Defense League of Halstead, Kansas. The list continues: The National Agricultural Press Association of Brighton, Colorado, Possess Comitatus of Tigerton, Wisconsin and the Iowa Society for Educated Citizens which meets at the Amanas.

These groups practice the art of scapegoating. In their anger, fear and rage, in their powerlessness they seek to blame and they are spreading the ancient vitriolic philosophy of anti-Semitism. They are telling people there is a Jewish based conspiracy to take over the nation's economy, including Iowa farms.

Fear filters down to the schools in towns like Wauzeka, Wisconsin where some parents have forced the Board of Education to cancel a school play based on the book, Workings by Studs Terkel.

One of the dangers running through this culture of fear is that people are willing to run after individuals, groups and systems of government which trade the pain of freedom, reason, choices, insecurity, for the "security" of censorship, restriction of dissent, setting aside the due process of law, for absolving oneself from responsibility. That form of security is nothing less than slavery.

To yield to this climate of fear is to cast a vote of no confidence in each other to deal with these situations in a reasonable manner. To yield is to nurture a breakdown of community.

Fear has to be given an outlet for expression as do powerlessness and even rage. By joining the hate mongers, spreading anti-Semitic philosophies, remaining silent in the face of bigotry, becoming violent in one's frustration: these will prove to be nothing but destructive. The hate-mongers have to be opposed whether they speak from the basement of a school or from the pulpit in a church.

Face the fears! Becoming paralyzed by them will only lead to self-destruction and the breakdown of a civilized, orderly society.

Indeed, there is nothing to fear but fear itself.

The Rise and Fall of the Religious Right

NOW
July 25, 2015

In this political year with an unprecedented number of candidates seeking to be elected President of the United States the "fear card" is being played. Since the attack on the World Trade Towers in 2001 the country has lived with a low level of fear, much like a low level of a fever. Add to that residual fear the increase of terrorist's activities which have become so prevalent since 2001: Madrid, London, Boston, Paris; gun violence reaching epidemic proportion with 200 plus mass killings (more than 4 persons killed or injured at one place), in the United States the latest being a rampage in Lafayette, La. which followed fast upon the killing of 9 worshipers at Emmanuel African Episcopal Methodist Church in Charleston, N. C.; Add to this the difficult economic times in the last 8 years, changes occurring within the social order: these are fear generating and unfortunately being exploited by the candidates seeking the 2016 election to the office of the presidency. To believe we have nothing to fear but fear itself requires holding on to one's faith tradition and believe that the goodness within will prevail.

THEN
The Rise and Fall of the Religious Right
August 3, 1982

While it would be premature to do a post mortem on the new right's alliance of "conservative religion and conservative politics," it is accurate to say the grip of this coalition on the tiller of the ship of state is weakening.

As Carol Flake recently pointed out in the *New Republic*, "It has become evident that the coalition between the religious right and secular right was a marriage of convenience and not of compatibility."

All about us there are signs of dissolution and the weakening of the grip on the tiller.

There is Nothing New Under the Sun

1. The recent decision of the Arkansas Supreme Court prohibiting teaching of "Scientific Creationism" in the public schools.
2. The appointment of Sandra O'Conner to the U. S. Supreme Court.
3. President Reagan's backing away from the granting of tax exempt status to segregated "Christian School."
4. The extension of the voting rights bill.
5. The waning in influence of "the electronic kingdom," i.e. television broadcasting. That's right: waning of influence even though the religious right claims television as its turf. All may not be well in its own backyard.

Let's look more closely at the "electronic kingdom" to ascertain the rise or fall of the "new right."

When we compare the 1982 convention of the national religious broadcasters with the 1981 convention we see important differences. In 1981 the convention was held in cooperation with the National Association of Evangelicals. The prayer breakfast held in conjunction with that gathering was attended by some 70 congressmen and senators. Jerry Falwell was the center of attention even though Billy Graham gave the major address which incidentally was received with subdued applause.

The 1982 convention was held separately from the National Association of Evangelicals. Jerry Falwell held but one brief press conference. Only a handful of politicians were present although President Reagan did make an appearance. The concerns of the convention dealt with television trade talk: ratings, the latest technology, promotion, etc.

The considerable divergence of points of view surfaced at this convention. For example: Mississippi United Methodist Donald Wildmon of the Coalition for Better television announced a spring boycott against sponsors of offensive television shows. Yet, a few days before Jerry Falwell declared he was "temporarily satisfied with the network's efforts to clean up the shows." Rex Humbard heeded Billy Graham's warning of 1981 about pride and becoming

The Rise and Fall of the Religious Right

too closely aligned with a political grouping and has backed out of the political arena. The same note was sounded by Jim Baker of the PTL club.

They discussed extensively the question of their religious shows becoming too entertaining and thus muting the message in the midst of the theatrics. James Robison of Dallas raised that question which could be easily personified by Rex Humbard. Pat Robertson of the 700 club might find that question discomforting as well. Even Billy Graham has made changes in his "Hour of Decision" focusing occasionally on the witness of celebrities.

Another sign of waning influence seemed to be the discrepancies noted between the ratings and revenue of National Religious Broadcast and those by independent study groups. The popular religious shows are losing over 6% of its viewers annually and they are experiencing financial difficulties. At the convention it became obvious that not all keep the faith in the same way nor are they all engaged in the same battles.

Yes, it is too early for a post mortem but it is safe to suggest the alliance is breaking up. The political and religious marriage is drifting towards dissolution. That is the signal I get from across the land. In my judgment the dissolution of that political and religious marriage could be a healthy thing for both religion and politics.

NOW
The Religious/Political Right
July 14, 2015

Note the New York Times articles focusing on the 15 Republican candidates giving a nod to the "evangelical vote" in their rhetoric focusing on same-sex marriage, immigration and the nuclear test ban treaty with Iran. Note in particular Bobby Jindal, Scott Walker and Donald Trump. Bobby Jingdahl would consider pushing for a constitutional amendment to preserve the status of marriage for heterosexual couples in the light of the Supreme Court's recent ruling endorsing same sex marriage.

There is Nothing New Under the Sun

In the May 27, 2015 issue of the Portland Observer we find this intimate relationship between the GOP presidential candidates and the religious right. David Lane, GOP operative who has GOP presidential candidates flocking to his meet-and-greets with conservative pastors has said Christians in America "Must risk martyrdom" over marriage equality. This, of course was a reference to same sex marriage being legalized by the Supreme Court.

THEN

Disinformation
April 15, 1985

The Greek writer of tragedies, Aeschylus has stated "In war, truth is the first casualty." As I read the news coming out of Washington, D. C. these days Aeschylus' comment comes to mind with a slightly different twist. In the foreign policy of this administration truth is the first casualty. The following inform my conclusion.

In an interview on April 1st President Reagan acknowledged that his policies towards Nicaragua are unpopular with Congress and the public, but blamed this on the "very sophisticated lobbying campaign by the Sandinistas and their Soviet and Cuban backers."

He goes on: "There has been a disinformation program that is virtually worldwide and we know the Soviets and the Cubans have such a disinformation network that is beyond anything that we can catch."

Although first reading suggests this to be a smokescreen of political gobbledygook aimed at confusing the public, which it probably does, I checked to see if such a word existed. I could not find it in two dictionaries, but I pieced the meaning of , two words together to see if understanding could be found: Dis and information.

Dis indicates negation, invalidation.

Information is defined as being informed, knowledge derived from study, experience and instruction.

Disinformation

Mr. Reagan is correct. Information brought back by 100,000 U. S. citizens and others who have lived for periods of time in Nicaragua, who have studied there, examined the history of the region are in fact, invalidating the Reagan administration's position. These informed citizens and students of the area are helping us to pursue truth, the first casualty in our foreign policy.

Item #2—In his recent press conference he was asked if he planned to visit a concentration camp while in West Germany next month. His reply:

"Instead of reawakening memories . . . maybe we should observe this day as the day when 40 years ago peace began and friendship. . .I felt since the German people have very few alive that remember even the war and certainly none of them who were adults and participating in any way, they have a feeling and a guilt feeling that's been imposed on them." (Register, April 9, page 6A)

The insight of Aeschylus seems so appropriate.

The man seems to be attempting to control history. His ability to add is called into question. More tragically he forgets that while there may be a statute of limitation on national guilt, there is no such statute on remembering. We all have that responsibility, including the people of West Germany. The memory of the victim is insulted by Reagan's refusal.

Item #3—Finally, we have the latest violation of conscience, truth and history. On April 11th the President said he would visit a cemetery of German soldiers while visiting in May and lay a wreath on their graves.

With the statement of Aeschylus in mind I ask myself: "How can this be?" Could this be 1984 in 1985? Is truth going down the memory hole? Is history being rewritten? One gets the impression the victims of the Holocaust are becoming the guilty ones and the Nazis are the ones being honored.

How can it be? One begins to question Mr. Reagan's reasoning ability, certainly his capacity to be sensitive, most assuredly his world view.

There is Nothing New Under the Sun

Aeschylus, we are in your debt in these days when "truth" is indeed becoming a casualty in our time. Thank you for the reminder which calls us to be aware.

NOW
Disinformation
July 14, 2015

Although the accusation of "disinformation" was used to try to discredit those protesting our involvement in Nicaragua now the term can be turned against those who have been spreading falsehoods, and negative innuendo around by opponents of the Affordable Care Act. The critics spoke of "death panels" when referencing the idea of patients visiting with their physicians about end of life issues. It seems that the current political campaign thrives on the spread of disinformation if not outright lies.

THEN
Bumper Stickers & Prejudice
1985

As I drive about the city I am accosted by a variety of messages from the rear bumpers of automobiles. You've seen them. Some are political: "The ERA is here to stay," "Support the Human Race, not the Arms Race," "Ban Handguns," or conversely, "When guns are outlawed only outlaws will have guns." There is counsel for the family. "Have you hugged your kids today?" Public service announcements are there as well: "Support your public schools." You have all seen those which say "I love blank (Iowa, N. Y., cats, dogs, etc.). The majority of these one can read and smile, shake one's head in agreement or disagreement and forget.

In recent months I have seen some which leave me with a feeling of discomfort. The target of these is presumably the economic scene but they convey a more insidious message. These

Bumper Stickers & Prejudice

stickers say this: "Unemployed. Made in Japan," and "Hungry? Eat your foreign car."

I know, the second one is a protest against the foreign car market even if it is not fully understood. One might say the message itself doesn't make sense. But the first one is very clear about its target. It too is a one line commentary on the economic conditions but it panders to our latent prejudice towards Americans of Asian ancestry.

In my judgment it begins to sound like the rhetoric surrounding analysis of the causes of WWII, blaming a group of people, namely the Jews for the economic plight of the world. We are subtly blaming the Japanese for our economic plight.

This blaming finds graphic demonstration in the behavior of people outside the auto plant in Detroit where on several occasions the unions would raise money for their members by charging people for the opportunity to take a sledge hammer to a Toyota. A harmless gesture? Perhaps? But I'm not convinced. It reinforces the idea of blaming the Japanese for our woes.

My discomfort may be exaggerated but my awareness of how we treat Asians has been sharpened in recent months by the review of our involvement in Vietnam when the memorial to the Americans killed in the war was unveiled.

It has been heightened by the current interest in the treatment of Americans of Japanese ancestry during World War II. There is almost unanimous outrage in our time over the treatment of these people on the West Coast in 1943 when Executive Order 9006 directed them to be placed in "internment camps," later called "concentration camps" by President Roosevelt.

Am I straining to make a connection? Of course no connection can be made between the bumper sticker and events 40 years previously, but I think it is appropriate to connect attitudes which permit that type of persecution to take place. A bumper sticker is a small thing; so is the smashing of a Toyota in Detroit. But news reports have revealed the subtle persecution which our fellow Americans of Japanese ancestry are experiencing on the West Coast today. And the tensions may increase.

There is Nothing New Under the Sun

Today we are experiencing what some commentators call the "Japanning of America." We know of their involvement in the auto industry. We have a Honda plant in Marysville, Ohio, Nissan—Datsun mini truck plant in Smyrna, Tenn., and the proposed joint venture between Toyota and General Motors. The Japanese steel company NKK is negotiating to buy a steel mill from Ford in Dearborn, Michigan.

The problems involved in this are many, particularly in the area of labor-management relations. Perhaps imaginative responses can be forthcoming as these plants become a part of the American landscape.

The problem will be compounded if we do not resist the appeals to our lower nature and promote meanness as well as untruths through the small, subtle media of bumper stickers.

THEN
Baseball Revisited
July 7, 1983

Something is happening to me! I am becoming afflicted with a childhood disease. I am becoming a baseball fan once again. The last time I was interested in baseball the Dodgers were leaving Brooklyn. For me a funeral dirge with the whole sport of baseball accompanied their journey west.

I'm not sure what it is that brought to life this malady which seemed to be hibernating within me. But I have a strong suspicion it is directly related to the rise of another team with an inglorious record in recent years: The Chicago Cubs.

I know I've the fever when I find myself reading the league standings in the morning papers. I noticed a change when I began glancing at a televised game of the Cubs in mid-afternoon as they played at that inviting bit of Americana, Wrigley Field. I know the illness is at an advanced stage when, upon entering the house at the end of the day, I ask: "Did the Cubs win?"

Baseball Revisited

The ashes of the memories of childhood were fanned to life when I watched the team make exciting plays, barely holding on to substantial leads, losing by one or two runs over and over again. There is something intriguing about their playing on *real grass*. It is as though the entire ballpark is a symbol of defiance to that which is artificial; the turf, a symbol of defiance against the elements; no roofed dome, a symbol of defiance against the megabucks; the lights for night games, the building of a new stadium to hold 70, 80, or even 90,000 fans. Lightless, small (40,000) maximum size crowd excluding standing room; Wrigley Field calls me back to the baseball team of my youth; the Dodgers, the Brooklyn Dodgers.

I cannot overlook the totally biased reporting of Harry Carey and Steve Stone; the personal touch in an impersonal age. Where else is there a broadcaster leading the crowd in singing "take me out to the ball game. . ." Are there other commentators who "dedicate" a game to an elderly woman in Burlington, Iowa who broke her hip on the way to a 65th wedding anniversary.

I think I like what is happening to me as this childhood malady comes over me. This is a much needed rebirth for me, to take me away from the heavy agenda of so much of live . . . to enjoy playing again, even if it is vicariously.

Maybe I will become as interested in the baseball skills of Durham, Hall, Bowa, Cey, Buckner, Davis and others as I was in the magnificent playing of the "Bums:" Jackie Robinson, Billy Cox, Pee Wee Reese, Carl Furillo, Gil Hodges, the"Duke," Roy Campanella and the others.

The Boys of Summer, about whom Roger Kahn wrote, enhanced the days of my youth. The Chicago Cubs are adding a bit of playfulness and excitement to my present.

As I watch this team and others, the social battles fought by Jackie Robinson, Joe Black and other Dodgers seem a long way off. The teams of today are multinational, multicultural and multiracial. That too excites me.

All of this and more contribute towards my condition of baseball revisited. And I'm grateful. PLAY BALL!!!

THEN
Can the Traditional Family be Saved?
1985

Can the traditional family be saved? This question raises other questions.

What is the traditional family? Is the traditional family in need of being saved?

If it is, from what?

Well there is the nuclear family: mother, father, and children.

The traditional family is the same as the nuclear family but in the traditional family the mother is at home and the father is the one who the livelihood.

Trying to save the traditional family as defined seems to me to be an attempt to hold on to the past; a journey into the land of nostalgia. But nostalgia is filled with myths and legends and to many attempts to romanticize the past.

The question of survival of the traditional family surfaces because of the high profile of destructive forces beating upon it.

1. The alarm is sounded over the dissolution of so many marriages. Little discussion is heard over the creation of stepfamilies resulting from second marriages.
2. The alarm is sounded over the amount of domestic violence usually with the woman as the victim.
3. The alarm is sounded over the issue of child abuse.
4. The alarm is sounded over the increasing number of women trying to find their own sense of personhood and independence especially as it concerns their attempts to enter the job market.

Let us take a closer look at these four items and diffuse the anxiety around them.

Let us begin with the 4th alarm concerning the woman's attempt to find a place for women in our society. This is certainly bringing about change in the traditional family role structures.

Can the Traditional Family be Saved?

And this will undoubtedly place the "traditional family" in an even smaller minority position. Thirteen per cent of families fall in the category of the traditional family; parents, children and one wage earner. The other three items; dissolution of marriages, abuse of women and children: these are not new, nor will they spell the end of the nuclear family.

History reminds us that instead of divorce in the "old days" we had "desertions." Men in particular could simply leave home, go to the frontier and start a new life. There were no legal agencies tracking them down. No social security numbers to trace. Desertion was prevalent rather than divorce. Desertion was prevalent rather than divorce. Domestic violence against women and children was common in the "old days." Women were abused even perhaps more overtly and with the "blessing of society," for men were definitely considered the "head" of the household which in many cases amounted to being "masters."

So called "good parents" often beat their children to "get the devil" out of them. Child abuse took many forms besides physical. When parents were working the children were often left in the care of older siblings or neighbors or permitted to run the streets freely.

The demands of the culture are definitely crowding the existence of the traditional family, with its specific role clarifications: woman in the home, man in the market place. The demise of this model may not be all bad when we remember the total dependency which goes along with this model, and the bondage in which so many women felt they lived and live in that mode.

The nuclear family; husband, wife and children, will survive although the roles change. The role change, the presence of domestic violence against women and children, serious though not new, will not mean the end of the nuclear family. It may diminish the traditional family where the husband works and the wife stays home.

In addition to the nuclear family we need to be sensitive to the other configurations of family life: single parent, communal arrangements, "stepfamilies", etc.

There is Nothing New Under the Sun

The question: Can the traditional family be saved? I'm not convinced it needs to be saved. It will continue to exist although its importance will diminish. It will not become extinct. The nuclear family will survive although roles will change. Other arrangements of family living are on the horizon, about which judgment needs to be reserved. The question for us is how do we cope with change and deal creatively with it to the enhancement of the wellbeing of all: women, children and men.

NOW
The Family Today
July 17, 2015

Since the early 80's the configuration of the reality called family has changed. The concerns of domestic abuse and child abuse have been brought to the front page of the news and programs to combat these two painful realities have become commonplace. In addition to programs dealing with the concerns noted in 1985 we have a great number of single parents (mostly women), women shattering the "glass ceiling" in the marketplace, gay and lesbian couples are becoming a familiar sight on our cultural horizons including television shows such as Modern Family. In 2004 it was reported in the New York Times, there were approximately 600,000 (reported) same gender households in the United States. Sixty thousand (60,000) of those were Lesbian households with children. Fifteen thousand (15,000) of those were households of gay men with children. At a minimum that was 75,000 households with children. Eleven years later one can assume the numbers are considerably larger.

Change has come and attempts to "push back" society's clock to the previous understanding of family have been resisted. The family has change and in my view for the better.

What follows is my personal testimony to the change in family structure in which the traditional roles of man and woman are reversed. After marriage in 2010 I found myself in the role of a full time homemaker while my wife worded full time. I found myself in the place of a woman. Since I write poetry, I put that awareness in the form of a poem.

In Place of a Woman

I am being called to a new place,
the place into which women have been
called for generations.
A place they have been
socialized to inhabit.
Following their partners,
Their husbands,
Their lovers
As they changed a new job
A new adventure,
A dream,
A whim,
From here, to there, to there.
I am being called to change,
To leave the familiar,
The secure,
The comfortable routine
The friends,
Following the call of love,
the holy.
Following is accompanied by the companions
of excitement,
Adventure,
Anxiety.
"Whither thou goest I will go",
Ruth spoke to Naomi long ago.
Today I am making that
statement of affection mine.
Not to find a refuge in a foreign land,
but to be a companion to a loved one.

"Whither thou goest, I will go"

There is Nothing New Under the Sun

That new place has found me in the role of a homemaker involving household chores and even discovering that I can bake pies as well.

THEN
"To Burn or Not to Burn"
March 9, 1983

It has happened again. At Greensburg, Pa. a group of young people billed as a "Christian Youth Group" has put the torch to about 100 "rock albums and tapes."

Records burned included the works of Stevie Wonder, The Rolling Stones, Kiss and Lynrd Skynrd as well as some country music and Lawrence Welk albums.

A few months ago a group in Iowa had a record burning. Included in the celluloid fuel were records by Perry Como. Not knowing what standards are used to determine what to burn or not to burn, I find it intriguing that records by Lawrence Welk and Perry Como qualify for the burning.

However, it is not the standards for choosing which to burn or not to burn that concerns me so much as what is done and why. Are these young people attempting to make a witness for some higher values? Letting their light shine as it were? (No Pun intended) Does this particular expression of protest contain dangerous aspects?

My reaction comes from a danger I see implicit in this kind of behavior. Burning records is like burning books. When books are burned, ideals are burned and can the authors be far behind? As I think about this record burning I must realize it may not be the ideas which call for the burnings. It could be the album covers which some people try to interpret in terms of the occult. Perhaps it's the music style. Unfortunately, there are people around who see these records as part of demonology, the occult, and the black arts.

In the records I've reviewed I fall to see the music, the lyrics or the covers as being worthy of burning. Some do not appeal to my particular taste in words or music, but that is a matter of personal preference. And a cover or two might be called "indelicate" in its graphics, but not something worthy of being put to the torch. As a matter of fact as I looked at the lyrics and listened to some of the orchestrations, I found them intriguing. I looked at and listened to the Rush album entitled "Moving Pictures" and I found the lyrics powerful, particularly the song "Witch Hunt." This is not a litany for the occult. It is a challenge to bigotry, prejudice, and intolerance. It speaks of vigilantes: their self-righteousness, their hatred for anything not like them, their desire to censor everything to do not like. Here I dub in music/words.

> Quick to judge, quick to anger
> Slow to understand.
> Ignorance and prejudice
> And fear walk hand in hand.

Did you hear the words?

To burn or not to burn? That is a question which must be weighed carefully.

THEN
A State of Minds
1982–1985

There are philosophers in state government. That truth leaped out at me in the form of the governor's recommendation and the Iowa Transportation Commission's promotion of a slogan for the 1985 Iowa license plates:

Iowa—A State of Minds

Don't let the idea of the presence of philosophers in state government frighten you. This proposed action and the slogan tell me that Iowa is a "think person's government."

I don't think the critics appreciate the philosophical theory being promoted by our leaders. But there is. That is the "Mind-Dust Theory." That theory tells us the individual mind results from

There is Nothing New Under the Sun

the combination of particles or mind which have always existed in association with material atoms." (1)

Translation: where there are particles of matter:; dust, dirt, trees, houses, etc, there are particles of mind. Since Iowa has a lot of these material atoms from dirt to houses and packing houses; it follows it has a lot of particles of mind.

The Iowa Transportation Commission, the Iowa Development Commission and the governor have uncovered one of the deep dark secrets of philosophical inquiry: the origin of the mind. It is in the good earth among the other particles of matter in our state.

What a discovery! The origin of the mind lies in the soil. This slogan: "A State of Minds" is a classy one. In the light of the "Mind-Dust Theory" it encompasses both agriculture and industry. One can also throw in the arts as well as education. There is no limit to the application of this slogan with that philosophical theory to support it.

> Arkansas can have its "Land of Opportunity",
>
> New Hampshire its "Live Free or Die",
>
> West Virginia—"Wild, Wonderful"
>
> New York—"The Empire State"
>
> Georgia—"The Peach State"
>
> Nebraska—"The Beef State"
>
> Minnesota—"10,000 Lakes"
>
> Missouri—"The Show Me State'
>
> Illinois—"The Land of Lincoln"

How common! How pedestrian! No class! No panache!

People expect a state slogan to portray a product, or a great citizen, even a flower or a bird, or a grandiose, patriotic slogan. But a School of Philosophy???

"The Mind-Dust Theory," long may it ride.

Anyway, I like the color.

Conclusion

Dogobert D. Runes, editor, Dictionary of Philosophy (Ames, Iowa: Littlefield, Adams & company., 1956), page 198

Conclusion
"Is there anything new under the sun?"

After viewing from the vantage point of some 35 years, a select number of issues from the 80s and comparing the manner in which those issues and concerns have been addressed in recent years, it is good to return to the question posed by the Preacher in Ecclesiastes. Qohelet, Hebrew for one who teaches the people and is aware of his world. As *The New Interpreter's Study Bible* tells us, he is considered a "practical theologian" who "honestly reflects on the ways of God in the world in order to instruct the people on how they should live."

With that biographical caveat we can say the Book of Ecclesiastes contains constants, variables which are unchanging because they portray human behavior. What does change is how we live out these variables and in the living impact the social fabric of society.

Here the Preacher!

> For everything there is a season, and a time for every matter under heaven:
> A time to be born, and a time to die;
> A time to plant, and a time to pluck up what is planted;
> A time to kill, and a time to heal;
> A time to break down, and a time to build up;
> A time to weep, and a time to laugh;
> A time to mourn, and a time to dance;
> A time to throw away stones, and a time to gather stones together;
> A time to embrace, and a time to refrain from embracing;
> A time to seek, and a time to lose;
> A time to keep, and a time to throw away;
> A time to tear, and a time to sew;

There is Nothing New Under the Sun

> A time to keep silence, and a time to speak;
> A time to love, and a time to hate;
> A time for way, and a time for peace.
> (Ecclesiastes 3:1–8)

What is new are the players, the actions, the play which is carried out on the stage of history. This is a production we have the privilege of attending as the variables of Ecclesiastes have been acted out in the 80's and now in the first decades of the 21st century.

When all is said and done for the moment, the Preacher has the final word indeed.

"Vanity of vanity, all is vanity!"